MANAGING
THE UNMANAGEABLE

MANAGING THE UNMANAGEABLE

Strategies for Success Within the Conglomerate

MILTON LEONTIADES

ADDISON–WESLEY PUBLISHING COMPANY, INC.

Reading, Massachusetts   Menlo Park, California
Don Mills, Ontario   Wokingham, England
Amsterdam   Sydney   Singapore   Tokyo
Mexico City   Bogotá   Santiago   San Juan

Library of Congress Cataloging-in-Publication Data

Leontiades, Milton.
  Managing the unmanageable.

  Includes index.
  1. Conglomerate corporations—Management.
I. Title.
HD2756.L46   1986   658'.046   85-11262
ISBN 0-201-15595-8

Cover design by Marshall Henrichs
Text design by Anna Post, Cambridge, MA
Set in 11 point Goudy Old Style by General Graphic Services, Inc., York, PA
ABCDEFGHIJ-DO-865
First printing, November 1985

— To —
Susan

CONTENTS

Part One

UNDERSTANDING THE CONGLOMERATE

1 WHY CONGLOMERATES GET NO RESPECT

I N THE LITERATURE of management, conglomerates have never been popular. The term itself invites skepticism. Conglomerates have been loosely defined as "a mass of parts from various sources." But even this description seems benign in comparison to the apparent havoc wreaked by some conglomerates that are haphazard at best, and incompatible at worst.

The formal definition of a conglomerate merger used by the Federal Trade Commission in 1969 was "the union of two companies having neither a buyer-seller relationship in manufacturing or distribution." The commission went on to illustrate such a union by the unlikely merger of "a ship builder and an ice cream manufacturer." Needless to say, this image did not build confidence in the inherent logic of conglomerating. What sense did it make for an ice-cream manufacturer and a ship builder, or a laundromat and bicycle producer, or a fast-food chain and a steel mill, or any such wild combination to merge into a single firm? Where was the synergy in such unions? How could these unwieldy structures be managed? Weren't companies challenged enough by the competitive battles within their own industry without undertaking the formidable task of managing businesses in completely different industries?

To be sure, the conglomerate record provides its critics with ammunition. Efficient management of conglomerates has proven elusive. Strategic planning often is a missing ingredient. These and other shortcomings have been microscopically reported in the negative reviews they have received by scholars and professionals alike. Yet the move into unrelated businesses continues, as shown in the following figure. Year after year since the mid-1950s, the trend to an increasing diversity among U.S. corporations has persisted. Today, less than fifteen percent of the *Fortune 500* companies remain largely in a single business. Recent unrelated acquisitions by newcomers like Goodyear, Coca-Cola, and General Motors almost assures that the level of diversification will continue to rise in the future. Indeed, it is increasingly difficult to pick up a newspaper or business magazine nowadays without reading about a takeover attempt by a large firm of a smaller, unrelated one.

The drive by companies into different lines of business has fundamentally changed the way companies operate. Not since multiple mergers created giant companies around the turn of the century — like U.S. Steel, American Tobacco, International Paper, U.S. Rubber, and others — has change been so dramatic. Yet amid all this change, the experts have had

**Large Acquisitions in Manufacturing and Mining
(By Type of Acquisition)**

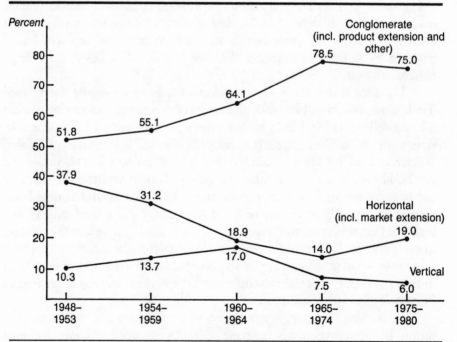

Source: Bureau of Economics, Federal Trade Commission, and author's interpolations of data. This government source was discontinued for years after 1980.

little advice to give corporate managers. How should companies position themselves to benefit from this reordering of assets? What types of synergy can be expected? How does management of several businesses differ from specialization in a particular industry? When must companies shift from routine to creative planning? By and large, managers have had to learn the answers to these questions through trial and error. And error in diversifying into unknown business territory can be fatal. Progress on developing a systematic approach to unrelated diversification has been distressingly modest.

To a manager, the conflict between practice and theory with regard to how conglomerates work must be baffling. Here is a strategy repeatedly confirmed by the actions of large numbers of firms for over three decades. Evolving from its revolutionary days during the 1950s and 1960s, unrelated diversification is now accepted in principle by some of the largest, most conservative, and most successfully managed companies in the nation. But the reasons underlying the strategy are as obscure as ever. Despite the added evidence every year brings that there is something right about conglomerates, the majority of expert opinion remains skeptical. Are businesspeople being deceived?

This book views conglomerates in a positive manner. It accepts the sustained conglomerate-style diversification for more than thirty years following World War II as evidence that the strategy is legitimate. It does not, in other words, seem necessary to build a completely new case *for* conglomerates in order to accept them as a permanent new dimension of business. Companies like Sears and Coca-Cola are not going to *undiversify*. Restructuring of the industrial population will continue. The relevant issues to address now include ways to handle diversity, given all the complexities associated with unrelated diversification. Answers are urgently needed by managers, while the merits of conglomerates can continue to be debated by scholars. The main purpose of this book is to help managers understand and deal with the special problem of diversity and improve the odds for making successful unrelated acquisitions when they're desired. But the first step in making "unmanageable" conglomerates manageable is to look beyond the often negative assumptions that have surrounded them for decades.

AN UNSHAKEABLE NOTION

John Kenneth Galbraith once observed that "the hallmark of conventional wisdom is acceptability." An idea widely shared is not easily rejected. The notion that conglomerates work represents only a very small fraction of scholarly and professional opinion. Currently opposition to the idea of conglomerates is largely instinctive, just as it was when giant enterprises were created by mergers around the beginning of this century. At that time, such mergers contradicted a preferred version of many small firms furthering competition among themselves. Giant firms could not be controlled, it was claimed. Today no one takes seriously the vision of an economy of miniscule firms, none of which can ultimately control their futures. In its place, the complexity of diversity represents a new challenge to conventional wisdom.

If you must diversify, stick close to what you know. This is a principal message of the popular book *In Search of Excellence,* and it reflects an opinion held by many others. Peters and Waterman, its authors, are obviously suspicious of conglomerates. Yet as an example of superior management they cite perhaps the most diversified company in the world: General Electric. Their explanation is that General Electric's businesses are "related." The crossover from the electric generating turbine to the jet engine (another turbine) is the example given to illustrate relatedness. What is left unmentioned was General Electric's manufacture of light bulbs, refrigerators, TVs, locomotives, and engineered plastics; its lease financing and computer services businesses; and its construction and engineering services. Clearly, GE has expanded into many types of businesses over the years, not all of them related, and has managed to integrate its various parts into a highly successful conglomerate.

What Peters and Waterman do is try to distinguish between "good" and "bad" conglomerates based on a uniquely personal perspective. As a further example, they give the illustration of Minnesota Mining and Manufacturing's (3M) expertise in coating and bonding technology as enabling it to "relate" to its unlike businesses of printing plates, microfilm systems, copying machines, abrasives and adhesives, and specialty chemicals. Admittedly, there is *some* degree of technology required for participation in these markets. But does a similarity in "coating and bonding technology" outweigh all the major differences among 3M's businesses?

A Question of Definition

One of the difficulties with assessing what's good and bad about unrelated diversification is that the very definition of the term *conglomerate* remains murky. *Fortune* labels companies as conglomerates if they operate in at least four unrelated businesses, none of which accounts for more than fifty percent of sales. Under this definition, both GE and 3M qualify as conglomerates. *Forbes* also uses "four sizable and distinct lines of business" as a measure of diversification. The Federal Trade Commission and the Securities and Exchange Commission similarly measure diversity based on the different businesses in which a firm competes, using the federal government's Standard Industrial Classification (SIC) system, which assigns every industry — from small to large — a specific code.

How diversified a company must become before it is considered a conglomerate is a matter of interpretation. There is no universal definition. The examples in this book include companies that have made major conglomerate-type acquisitions which meet the FTC's criterion of "neither company having a buyer-seller relationship nor a functional relationship in manufacturing or distribution." This casts a wide net, covering companies that may not be termed "conglomerates" according to a stricter rule. However, the objective here is not to develop consensus on a definition, but to describe the various possibilities.

Hence Sears is viewed as a conglomerate because it participates in at least four distinct businesses: retailing, insurance, real estate, and financial securities. Similarly, R. J. Reynolds Industries operates in more than four different parts of the food and beverage industries — even though over fifty percent of sales still come from tobacco — and thus it must deal with all the problems of unrelated diversification. Finally, companies like General Motors, Coca-Cola, and Goodyear have made major conglomerate-type acquisitions, and their managements have expressed interest in further diversification. Each of these companies therefore has endorsed the concept of unrelated diversification. The differences between them and more complex conglomerates are ones of degree rather than philosophy. Whether simple or complex, the problems that unrelated diversification raises will have to be overcome.

CONGLOMERATES: SPECIAL CASES, SPECIAL SOLUTIONS

Although a great deal of effort might be expended debating the critics of conglomerates, an affirmative case *for* conglomerates must explain how synergy or value arises from combining unlike businesses. How can companies with no apparent commonalities be more profitable together than separately? In fact, there are several types of synergies that can be obtained from diversifying into unrelated businesses, depending on the resources or distinctive competences a company has to devote to its acquisitions (see Chapter 3). The more resources, the more synergy a company can expect from the combination. For example, a firm with only financial resources to bring to an acquisition can expect relatively modest success, since the acquired company will operate at the same level of efficiency as before its purchase. On the other hand, a company with the administrative capacity to restructure, integrate, and manage its acquisitions can aspire to a higher order of synergy — if it is willing to undertake the greater risks.

Distinctive competences — specific functional skills, from marketing, production, and technology, to managerial innovation and efficiency — are not equally distributed among businesses. Thus, it is imperative that a company have an intimate knowledge of its own distinctive skills and limitations, and apply them realistically in striving for synergy in its diversification program. The knack is knowing when to diversify, what to diversify into, and being able to integrate the new businesses. An increasing number of companies have taken the first step. Some have had a measure of success with the second. What remains to be shown is whether the parts of a conglomerate can be operated as a unified organization. Without the transition from the entrepreneurial moves of active diversification to professional administration of the whole, firms will stop short of becoming mature and successful conglomerates.

The Management Challenge

Handling the sheer size of multi-billion-dollar corporations poses an immense challenge. How can firms be expected to manage the added dimension of unrelatedness? This commonly asked question raises doubts about the ability of conglomerates to compete. While it is a valid point, the problem is not unsolvable. A part of the answer is time. The art of managing conglomerates takes years — perhaps generations — to perfect. This accounts for the fact that so few conglomerates or aspiring conglomerates have been totally successful. Such success involves a considerable period of experimentation, perhaps more than one cycle of restructuring, and luck. Time and judicial transitional strategies are crucial elements of success.

Specific suggestions for successful management deal with the development of new organizational structure, cultivating distinctive competences, and choosing the right managers to fit the strategy. These issues are discussed in greater detail in Part II of this book. Each topic involves an area needing reform. An active diversifier, for example, tries to balance two objectives: to optimize internal growth while trying to grow externally through acquisitions. Managing both types of strategies means simultaneously building flexibility and cohesiveness within a company. This means rethinking the conventional structures designed for managing size alone and developing new linkages between the corporate level and the operating divisions.

Building a distinctive competence is another ingredient for success. While most of the experts reinforce the importance of specialization within an industry, conglomerates by definition try to transfer skills into *different* industries. This emphasizes the advantages of *scope* over those of *specialization,* and the value of cultivating distinctive skills in order to make the successful crossover into a new business. Here again, new ideas to implement the new strategy are sorely needed by managers.

Also, as diversifying companies acquire new businesses and cultures, a change in managerial styles becomes an issue. Choosing managers that complement a company's strategy is a logical proposition. What eludes many companies is its proper execution. Well-articulated theories of management selection exist side-by-side with many real situations of the wrong person promoted to the wrong job.

The Building Challenge

Before a conglomerate can be managed it must be built. And success in the construction of a conglomerate depends in large measure on selecting the right businesses. Part III of this book views the importance of strategic planning to the diversification program, as well as knowing the business you are buying and limiting the number of acquisitions to a digestible pace.

To become a conglomerate, firms must deliberately *plan* to acquire unfamiliar businesses. In addition, they must develop planning systems to effectively control all the unrelated parts. Surveys have uncovered a groundswell of discontent with the results of strategic planning at the corporate level. In company after company, planning systems have been designed to primarily accomodate the divisions. Planning for corporate-wide change is largely an ad hoc exercise. Specifically, creative strategic planning — as opposed to the tactics of operational plans — is systematically pursued in only a few isolated cases.

The planning job is made easier when companies are familiar with the businesses they acquire and acquire only as many as they can handle. These are commonsense precautions. Yet they are repeatedly ignored. Success in almost every business, for instance, depends on grasping one or two "key" elements that are decisive for competing effectively. Identifying these "keys" is not always easy. But, surprisingly, many companies do not even try. A number of things can go wrong with even the best-planned acquisition. To attempt a successive series of major acquisitions dramatically increases the risk of failure.

HOW BIG BUSINESS GOT THAT WAY

The present debate over the merits of conglomerates would no doubt benefit from a closer examination of business history. Unrelated diversification is but a stage in a recurring pattern of resurgence and evolution. The tactics have changed, but the striving for growth and survival has remained a consistent force in business. It is as unlikely that the current trend toward unrelated diversification signals the last great change in this evolution as it was that companies would be content to produce only a single product, or market it only domestically, or not consolidate for economies of scale, or not branch into related products and markets. Correspondingly, the conflicting opinions on the conglomerate rationale eventually will be reconciled. If history is a guide, a look backward at today may make anxiety over the current predicament seem exaggerated.

Emergence and Growth (1850s to 1930s)

Before 1850 and the rise of "modern capitalism," basic management functions were exercised by a single owner, manager, financier, and principal decision-maker in typically small, local concerns. Neither great size nor explosive growth were realistic goals. Merchant firms were limited on both fronts by unreliable transportation and cumbersome communications systems. Not until railroads and telegraphy provided the catalysts for growth could firms expand rapidly and on a nationwide scope.

With the opening of new frontiers, the rush to expand was on. New markets created demand. Innovations in continuous-process machinery enabled volume production. High cash flows generated the profits for additional capacity. This market-driven cycle of expansion created the first mass producers, and set the pattern for other companies to emulate.

Size was the fundamental strategy. A consequence of size was investment in large plants, representing commitment to high volume output. This was effective as long as work flowed smoothly and demand kept pace with productive capacity. In some cases, assuring a smooth production flow meant extending a firm's reach beyond the manufacture of goods.

In distribution, for instance, networks of many small firms could not serve manufacturers many times their size. Wholesalers and distributors not prepared to meet manufacturers' special needs or adjust to their style of doing business were absorbed or bypassed. Meat packers like Armour, Cudahy, Morris, and Swift developed their own refrigerated transport systems in order to assure the quality of fresh meat shipped over great distances. In the beer industry, Anheuser-Busch, Blatz, Pabst, and Schlitz developed buying and marketing networks to serve their special needs. Similarly, food and produce companies integrated their operations from the growing of the bananas on plantations in the Caribbean, to shipping, to processing plants in the United States and throughout the world.

Unpredictable downturns in business posed another type of market uncertainty. With the depression of 1873, demand dropped sharply and prompted firms to bond together to protect themselves from ruinous price-cutting competition. At first this resulted in "gentlemen's agreements," or pools, to set prices and carve up markets. These pools relied on the co-operative efforts of many firms. But being unenforceable, these efforts failed as members caved in to the temptations of individual advantage.

But the desire to exert control over markets remained strong. Pools were followed by trusts, whereby ownership was vested in a board of trustees who accomplished through administrative control what had proved impossible through informal agreements. Although effective, this form of centralized control was soon declared illegal. Undeterred, companies turned to holding companies, which also allowed centralized control but avoided the "antitrust" laws. These holding companies formed the nucleus of the multi-company mergers that occurred around the turn of the century. These mergers for market power established the leaders within major industries, and characterized the next major phase of evolution.

The Merger Trend (1898 to 1903)

Having achieved efficiencies of large size, leading companies next sought greater market power within their industries. Organized into holding companies, they then moved to merge competing firms into one giant enterprise. These multiple mergers arose in almost every major industry. They offered the expediency of size without productive effort, and an increase in market power for the survivors. Dozens of smaller firms typically were combined in a simultaneous merger to create one much larger and stronger competitor. Such mergers were instrumental in the formation of modern-day giants like General Electric, DuPont, American Brands, National Brands, International Paper, U.S. Steel, and others.

Contributing to this urge to consolidate was the surge in stock market activity in industrial shares. Turning from railroad to industrial securities, financiers and promoters contributed to — and benefited from — the demand for such investments. In the process, a "new profession, that of merger promoter, arose."[1] The promotion of mergers was lucrative for the financial community and potentially rewarding for investors. Ownership of industrial stocks broadened, as it had in railroad securities previously, and stock ownership and managerial control eventually came to rest in separate groups.

Almost as quickly as it arose, however, the heated activity in mergers cooled off. The so-called richman's panic of 1903 dampened investors' enthusiasm by underlining the risks, as well as the profits, inherent in these heavily promoted combinations. Although a few important consolidations were still to come, they were not the driving force in future merger activity. That role was to be assumed by the acquisition type of merger.

The Rise of Related Acquisitions (1904 to 1930s)

Those industries earlier consolidating also tended to be those in which acquisitions were concentrated. An "acquisition" form of merger refers to the combination of two firms, with the larger generally absorbing the smaller. By contrast, the "consolidation" type of merger involved a simultaneous merger of many firms. The shift in merger patterns is summarized in the following table.

Distribution of Firm Disappearances by Type of Merger, 1895 – 1920 (%)

	1895 – 1904	1905 – 1914	1915 – 1920
Acquisitions and consolidations of two to four firms	25.0%	62.3	86.1
Consolidations of five or more firms	75.0	37.7	13.9

Source: Nelsen, Ralph L. Merger Movements in American Industry, 1895 – 1956, Princeton, N.J.: Princeton University Press, 1959, p. 53.

Overall, the acquisition type of merger tended to pick up where consolidations had left off. Both types of mergers helped companies strengthen their dominance within industries. Acquisitions allowed further consolidation of industry positions and eventual diversification into related products and markets.

In addition to acquisitions, companies looked to new product development for continued growth. The ability of mass production and mass distribution systems to handle additional products first led companies to a "full line" strategy. In some cases, this meant merely augmenting the product line. Meat packers, for example, expanded into poultry and dairy products as logical extensions of investments in refrigeration and storage facilities. Steel firms began to develop "lines" of products to specific customer specifications, in addition to the mass produced commodity-type metal products.

Another tactic was to develop new products through research and development. DuPont pioneered this type of strategy. Initially a manufacturer of explosives, DuPont diversified after World War I into paints, chemicals, artificial fibers, artificial leather, and celluloid film. Each new line relied on the same chemical technology involved in the manufacture of explosives. Companies like U.S. Rubber and B.F. Goodrich also applied their knowledge of chemistry to expand their product lines. By 1920, many technologically advanced companies had built extensive research facilities. It was no great leap for managers to utilize already committed resources to the development of new products, which would in turn utilize the distribution and administrative structures of the existing system.

In yet another push for growth, companies began to market products abroad. Many of the same large integrated firms dominating domestic sectors of the U.S. economy became the first multinationals. This was especially true of companies that were also skilled in marketing. Marketing networks were the first part of a strategy of foreign diversification, followed by investment in plant and equipment.

By the 1930s, big business was seen to be running out of options for continuing the growth rates of the past. The major battles for industry dominance had already been decided. Logical product and market extensions had occurred. Economists foresaw an indefinite period of relatively static equilibrium. While skirmishes for advantage within industries would continue, the battlefields themselves would not change. It was not until the second half of the twentieth century that this interpretation of evolution was to be proven wrong.

The Golden Age of Conglomerates
(1955 to 1968)

Beginning around the mid-1950s, a second major evolutionary shift by big business began. A radically different strategy of diversifying into unrelated businesses emerged. Instead of an industry-specific orientation, companies turned to multi-industry diversity. In essence, this new "conglomerate" philosophy offered a way to keep growing — providing a consistency with past events in one sense, but contradicting the notion of industrial stability as the vision of the future.

This Golden Age of unrelated diversification saw the emergence of a new type of manager — the conglomerate entrepreneurs. In many respects, they resembled the owner-entrepreneurs of the previous century. They were instinctive leaders. Lacking a formal organization design, they tended to dominate through sheer force of style. Decision-making was personalized rather than diffused through committees. As a group, they were less educated, less skilled in managing, and less inhibited by tradition than their business counterparts. They were clearly not professional administrators. Variously called macromanagers or empire builders, they have been likened to the old captains of industry like Ford, Rockefeller, and Carnegie. They obviously sought gratification from the challenge of creating an enterprise of their own making rather than heading up a large existing corporation.

This portrait corresponded to the conglomerate stereotype. It was an image developed and exaggerated by focusing on the most actively acquiring companies in this first "wave" of unrelated diversification. Old-line companies like General Electric, Westinghouse, Minnesota Mining and Manufacturing, and Koppers were never tagged as conglomerates. Their diversity had evolved over time and primarily by internal expansion. Although operating in several industries, they were set apart from the "new" conglomerates from the start. The "new" conglomerates, by contrast, were acquiring companies in unrelated fields at a feverish pace.

The historical record on these "new" conglomerates is in many respects an account of those individuals in the forefront of the movement. Representative of the chief executives in this group was James J. Ling, head of Ling-Temco-Vought (now LTV). Ling started with a modest $3,000 investment in an electrical contracting business in 1946. By 1959, he had acquired Temco Aircraft, a company with $100 million in sales and assets of $34.5 million. During 1961 to 1968, Ling's firm made twenty-three acquisitions, four of which had assets in excess of $100 million, including one company with over $1 billion in assets. Not bad for a company not in existence barely a decade earlier. Equally impressive was Gulf & Western's (now G + W) meteoric rise under the leadership of Charles Bluhdorn. Starting as a small auto-parts business in 1958, Gulf & Western by 1968 was the thirty-fourth largest industrial corporation in the *Fortune 500*, with interests in zinc, sugar, cigars, industrial products, motion pictures, paper products, musical instruments, publishing, real estate, insurance, and investment.

They were a flamboyant group, the Jimmy Lings and the Charles Bluhdorns. In its report on conglomerates, the Federal Trade Commission catalogued the exploits of eleven firms epitomizing this new breed of company, and included Ling-Temco-Vought, Gulf & Western, International Telephone and Telegraph, Teledyne, Litton, Food Machinery and Chemical, Textron, White Consolidated, and Colt Industries. These companies were singled out because their activities accounted for more than half the assets acquired by the twenty-five most active conglomerates during the 1960s (See the following table). A review of this list reinforces the conglomerate image of companies achieving phenomenal growth and complexity in a relatively short span of years.

Textron, Litton, Food Machinery and Chemical, Teledyne, and others studied by the Federal Trade Commission were described as companies resolved to grow before establishing a format for expansion. Indeed, with no historical precedence to guide them and no economic justification as support, trial and error in building these new multi-industry empires was inevitable. For strong-willed men of action, a carefully detailed and articulated plan of diversification would not have been in character. So haphazard, in fact, was their "program" of diversification that Textron, one of the first companies to piece together a true conglomerate successfully, observed in the late 1950s that it would devote "a large part of its energies into finding out just what it was doing right."[2]

One common characteristic of these conglomerate entrepreneurs was their bent towards the financial side of managing. Interestingly, this perspective is the one point on which conglomerate managers and their critics agreed, but with different interpretations. Stressing the negatives, critics saw conglomerateurs as empire-builders, "pushed by visions of creating a powerful industrial 'empire' extending over a wide area. . . . Many empire-builders are, as individuals, nothing more than financial speculators, and the collection of firms they acquire never take on the character of a single industrial firm."[3]

Conglomerate entrepreneurs agreed with a financial rationale for diversifying, seeing themselves as managers of pools of capital rather than as

New Conglomerates Among the Most Active Diversifiers in the 1960s*

Company	No. of Acquisitions 1961 – 1968	Large $50m. +	Acquisitions $10 – 49M	Date Started	Original Business	Pioneering Executives
Gulf & Western	67	10	3	1958	Auto Parts	Charles Bluhdorn
LTV	23	5	4	1958	Electronics Aerospace	James J. Ling
IT&T	47	7	9	1960	Telecommunications	Harold Geneen
Teledyne	127(1960 – 61)	3	11	1960	Electronics Aviation	Henry Singleton Geo. Kozmetsky
Litton	97(1958 – 69)	2	18	1953	Electronics	Chalres Thornton Roy Ash
FMC	NA	2	4	1928	Machinery	Paul Davies
Textron	70(1948 – 68)	NA	NA	1955	Textiles	Royal Little
White Consolidated	27	4	3	1964	Sewing Machines	E.S. Reddig
Colt Industries	NA	2	2	mid - 1950s	Machinery	Geo. Strichman

* Of eleven firms included by the FTC, GTE was omitted because it was a utility holding company whose acquisitions were mostly telephone companies, and GATX because it made the list due to a single large acquisition: LaSalle National Bank; subsequently divested.

Source: Federal Trade Commission, Bureau of Economics, "Economic Report of Corporate Mergers," *Hearings before the Subcommittee on Antitrust and Monopoly,* 1969, Chapter 8.

"manufacturers," or "marketeers," or "service businesses." In their opinion, money should be free to seek its highest return, regardless of industry. To many theorists, this violated the assumption that companies do best by sticking to the business they know. Instead of contesting this principle, conglomerates made it the corner stone of their strategy. As one chief executive put it: "The basic thing in this kind of operation is return on your invested capital. That's what this game is all about."[4] If returns could be maximized in industries other than those of the current business, this was all the justification needed. Royal Little, former chief executive of Textron and one of the most articulate proponents for the diversification strategy of conglomerates, stated the case succinctly:

> It has been shown that through the combination of normal internal growth, plus growth through unrelated business acquisitions, you can get better cumulative growth rate on capital than can be obtained in any normal, single-industry operation. That, I believe, is why unrelated diversification is here to stay, because you just can't beat it unless you're the one in a hundred thousand that comes up with Xerox or Polaroid.[5]

The peak of the Golden Age for conglomerates was the mid-1960s. Stock prices were up. Profits were up. A buoyant stock market was stimulating a record number of acquisitions and more and more acquisitions were of the "pure" conglomerate variety. Increasing numbers of companies were converting to the conglomerate point of view. In short, conglomerates were enjoying their success. While still lacking a formal justification for their strategy, they had become too pervasive a phenomenon to ignore. By comparison, one-industry blue-chip companies appeared lackluster. For the moment, critics of conglomerates, if not silenced, were at least muted.

A Period of Reevaluation (1969 to 1976)

But what goes up must come down. And in the late 1960s conglomerates began a descent from their peak. By 1968, a number of indicators turned from green to red. Litton, Gulf & Western, and Ling-Temco-Vought — all recording phenomenal increases in sales and earnings in the mid-1960s — either showed declines or decreases in growth rates for 1968. In 1969, the stock market turned sharply lower and continued depressed through the middle of 1970. Price-to-earnings ratios followed the decline in stock prices. Consequently, acquisitions made on a share-for-share basis when acquirors' shares were at a price-earnings premium now seemed less attractive. Investors drawn by the large gains to be made when the conglomerate movement was in vogue were just as eager to avoid a reversal of this trend as the market quickly slid back. For those investors and entrepreneurs hoping for a return to the ebullient environment of the 1960s, the next sharp break in the stock market in 1974 provided a final disillusionment. The climate had changed. The stock market was mirroring economic conditions that were to affect the character — although not the basic thrust and idea — of conglomeration.

Instead of acquiring, companies began to divest. Many companies found themselves unprepared to manage what had so rapidly been assembled. In 1970 alone, the number of divestments rose by 75 percent from 1969 (see the following table). The majority of divestments could be traced to those companies that had earlier been the active or "swinging" conglomerates. Having extended themselves when prospects appeared bright, these same conglomerates were forced by circumstances to reduce the costs of carrying acquisitions performing well below expectations.

Importance of Divestitures in the Acquisition and Merger Movement

Year	Divestitures	Net Mergers and Acquisition Announcements	Percent of Divestitures
1963	N/A	1361	—
1964	N/A	1950	—
1965	191	2125	9%
1966	264	2377	11
1967	328	2975	11
1968	557	4462	12
1969	801	6107	13
1970	1401	5152	27
1971	1920	4608	42
1972	1770	4801	37
1973	1557	4040	39
1974	1331	2861	47
1975	1236	2297	54
1976	1204	2276	53
1977	1002	2224	45
1978	820	2106	39
1979	752	2128	35
1980	666	1889	35
1981	830	2395	35
1982	875	2346	37
1983	932	2533	37
1984	900	2543	35

Source: W.T. Grimm and Co.

It is, however, a simplistic interpretation to attribute all divestments to faulty conglomerate logic and use this as the means for discrediting the entire movement. The effects of a declining stock market and worsening economic conditions reached far beyond the "swinging" conglomerates that came to represent the 1960s. Poor planning and poor execution plagued American companies in general, many of which were not of the conglomerate type.

The cases described below are illustrations of what went wrong in three situations. The first is Westinghouse, a diversified but old-line company that overreached, acquiring more than it was capable of digesting. The second case involves Storer Broadcasting's purchase of Northeast Airlines — a move attributable to naivete rather than greed. U.S. Industries (USI) provides the final example, chosen because it reflects the stereotyped excesses of random conglomeration at its worst.

Westinghouse

The ambitious manager had big plans for his small part of Westinghouse Electric Corp. Asked what his sales goal was, he replied, "We can do $800 million this year and get it up to $2 billion very quickly after that."

"That was the last official statement he ever made," says Robert E. Kirby, Westinghouse's new chairman, who fired the man shortly thereafter. . . . And now that Mr. Kirby is the top man at Westinghouse, he is busy spreading (the) gospel throughout the company. His approach is part of a new, get-tough, back-to-basics strategy that has taken hold at the country's fourteenth largest industrial company. That strategy has two goals. One is to halt this year the two-year earnings slide that sent Westinghouse's 1974 net profit skidding to only $28.1 million from a 1972 high of $198.7 million.

The other is to prevent the recurrence of a series of corporate foul-ups stemming from overambitious growth plans that cost Westinghouse millions of dollars in 1973 and 1974 and that at one point last year led, in Mr. Kirby's words, to a "vision of Westinghouse being pulled through a little knothole."

Not only is the company clamping down hard on managers who want to expand too fast, it has also been acting to prune away the mistakes of the past. Over the last few months Westinghouse has closed or sold five major money-losing operations that accounted for some 15 percent of its business in 1973. . . . The back-to-basics drive adds up to a sharp turn away from the direction that Westinghouse has been traveling since the early 1960s.[6]

Storer Broadcasting

Broadcasting is a virtual money machine. Broadcast licenses are limited by the Federal Communications Commission: Generally only four or five TV licenses are granted to a major metropolitan area. As a market city grows, a fixed supply of advertising time is overwhelmed by the demand for time.

On top of that, the stations have little in the way of fixed assets. Storer figures that its replacement costs for capital equipment run at less than 50% of depreciation, in contrast to most businesses in which depreciation runs below inflated replacement costs.

Moreover, where a major network must risk big bucks on a dozen new series, non-network-owned station operators like Storer need only produce local news, public affairs and children's programs; they then buy syndicated programming and use some network shows to complete their schedules. At close to the industry's average, Storer's programming costs are only 30 percent of net revenues. . . .

The big mistake that was to lead to Storer's fall from grace on Wall Street came in 1965. The FCC limits the number of stations in one ownership, and Storer had almost reached the limit. That gave him a problem: What do you do with your rich cash flow from earnings and depreciation when you can't expand in your own business and when that business doesn't require much capital?

Listening perhaps to some bad advice from the investment community, Storer went out and bought Northeast Airlines. He figures the excess cash from his broadcasting money machine could buy the short- and medium-range plans that Northeast's management thought it needed. Trouble was, Northeast was broke when Storer bought it, and the once-glamorous airline industry started a nosedive just a few years after Storer got into it. It took years to sell Northeast to Delta and to unwind the mess.[7]

U.S. Industries

The Sixties burst of corporate diversification — the decade that saw the emergence of the conglomerate — also made fashionable an extreme theory of decentralization: Buy companies with good managements and let them keep on running things. Such logic died a quick death in the turbulent Seventies, when divisional disasters forced many a multicompany to ride closer herd on its operations.

U.S. Industries is a classic example. . . . USI [was] the most conglomerated conglomerate of them all. It absorbed more than 100 smallish companies on the theory that it could help entrepreneurs to do better by giving them centralized staff assistance they could not afford on their own. Instead, it acquired a multitude of headaches that the USI staff couldn't begin to cope with. Now [1975], with four presidents in 14 months, the company is trying to consolidate 100 divisions into 27. "USI defies intelligent analysis," says portfolio manager (for Windsor and Gemini funds) John Neff, a former believer in USI.[8]

As the above casualties proved, there was still much to be learned about the merits and methods of venturing into unknown business territory. Yet even as the pieces were being picked up from these and other failures, companies began looking for the right opportunity to resume a strategy of unrelated diversification. An important difference this time was that managers would take a more cautious and planned approach to their futures.

The Emergence of Professional Managers
(1977 to mid-1980s)

In contrast to the newly emergent conglomerates of the 1960s — constructed haphazardly from modest beginnings and guided by the vision of a dominant chief executive — the third merger wave saw the entry of old-line, conservatively managed giants. Industrial titans like Mobil, Coca-Cola, Philip Morris, Goodyear, and U.S. Steel, as well as giant nonindustrial firms like American Express and Sears, placed their imprimatur on the concept of conglomerate-style diversification. No longer could the movement be tied to a few highly visible and radical companies.

In the first merger wave, DuPont's president had observed: "Running a conglomerate is a job for management geniuses, not for ordinary mortals like us at DuPont."[9] But by 1981, DuPont had acquired Conoco, the nation's eighth largest oil company. Giant one-industry firms like Anheuser-Busch (which acquired Campbell-Taggart, the nation's second largest bakery), U.S. Steel (which acquired Marathon Oil), Coca-Cola (which acquired Columbia Industries, a diversified entertainment company), and Sears (which acquired Coldwell Banker in real estate and Dean Witter in securities) moved to reposition their organizations into new businesses. Conservatively managed companies like Nabisco (which merged with Standard Brands to form National Brands) and Kraftco (which merged with Dart Industries to form Dart & Kraft) made their most significant diversification moves since the giant consolidations around the turn of this century. Exceptionally managed companies that had previously diversified primarily through internal means also became converts: Procter & Gamble acquired Norwich, a pharmaceutical firm, and Crush International, a soft-drink company. Even the railroads began to follow suit: Union Pacific acquired Champlin Petroleum and Burlington Northern acquired El Paso, a large natural gas pipeline company.

This blue-chip roster of reputable old-line firms added legitimacy to the idea of acquiring unrelated businesses. As *Forbes* aptly put it: "Conglomerates are no longer the scarlet women of America. Many of them are quite respectable matrons."[10] Conglomerates had come of age. The concept had survived an initial binge of random growth and a pause for digestion and divestment. What was eventually discredited was not the principle of unrelated diversification, but merely its unsound and unplanned application by some of the companies that had practiced it.

In this latest period, companies not only acquired new businesses, but they often exited from businesses that once had been their trademark. Variously termed "asset redeployment," "corporate restructuring," or "rationalization," it signaled nothing less than the rebirth of a firm. Corporate repositioning forced changes as dramatic for some companies as the turn-of-the-century mergers and consolidations that had created them. Such restructuring begs a question first posed in the early 1960s by Theodore Levitt of Harvard University: "What type of business do you want to be?" This inquiry was intended to stretch management's imagination beyond the confines of a particular product line. For example, railroads should not necessarily restrict themselves to railroading. In a larger sense they were in the transportation business, which would include a potentially wide variety of complementary businesses and services into which railroads might logically diversify. Similarly, computer firms could be deemed to be in the business of communications, and manufacturers of bowling equipment might be part of the leisure business.

Conglomerates stretch this perspective to the limit: if the business of business is to make money, then the search for profit could be expanded to include all markets, *unrestricted* by their relatedness to the existing business. In fact, this perspective was becoming a conspicuous part of strategy at more and more firms. The end result could — and did — lead to corporate renaissances.

NL Industries (the old National Lead Company), for example, is no longer connected with lead, its original product and one that identified the company's main line of business. Similarly, Westinghouse no longer manufactures major appliances or light bulbs. Esmark (built on the foundation of the old meat-packer, Swift & Co.) sold its fresh meat business (and itself was later acquired by Beatrice Foods). Allegheny International (formerly the Allegheny Ludlom Steel Co.) sold its specialty steel business. Harris (which started as a printing press manufacturer) has sold its printing equipment operations, and Insilco (the old International Silver Co.) has divested its silverware business. In each of these situations, the companies divested themselves of mature businesses identified with their corporate origins. Moreover, even while retaining "core" businesses, many diversified companies reduced the percent of total revenues attributable to this source to less than half of their revenues. Less reliance on a single business follows the pattern of early conglomerates, whose accumulated unrelated acquisitions successively reduced the weight of original product lines.

This massive redeployment has underlined the major shift in strategies. No longer do companies feel restricted by industry boundaries or committed to remain in current lines of business. Each business is viewed for its contribution to the total organization, with dollars redeployed if units no longer "fit" the strategic design, can no longer meet minimum performance standards, or if resources can be more profitably employed in other operations.

One result of this new strategy has been a blurring of industry boundaries. Classifications by Standard Industrial Classification (SIC) codes into electrical, paper, chemical, metal, and other "industries" are increasingly inappropriate. More and more, big business is operating a family of strategic groups that cut across several traditional industry sectors.

A Question of Survival

Looking back, we see that big businesses evolved in two fundamentally different ways. They grew big and then they diversified (see following figure). Within each phase there were similar patterns of adaptation. For example, in the first phase of movement companies sought volume, then consolidated, and then began growing again. After the second world war, companies began diversifying into unrelated fields by acquiring other companies. During all this time, a pattern of growth, consolidation, and renewed growth emerged.

In the first stage of evolution, expansion was contained within industry sectors. This situation would have led eventually to the static equilibrium

The Two Strategic Dimensions of Evolution

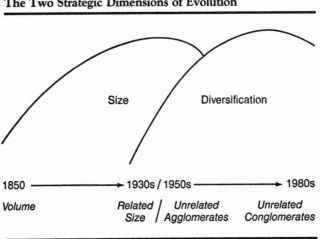

1850	1930s / 1950s	1980s
Volume	*Related* / *Unrelated*	*Unrelated*
	Size / *Agglomerates*	*Conglomerates*

that was foreseen. Yet within these bounded arenas the reasons for expansion, including new financial and functional synergies, remained as strong as ever. There was, in other words, a built-in conflict in this view of evolution.

The dilemma proved remarkably easy to solve. Conglomerate entrepreneurs simply ignored industry boundaries. Their strategy of multi-industry structures avoided the major impediment to growth. Now companies theoretically could grow to a size, and in a variety of different markets, previously thought to be impossible.

Henry Singleton, the founder and chief executive of Teledyne, a major conglomerate built in the 1960s, articulated the case for growth — and indirectly the drive — that led Teledyne and other conglomerates to a policy of unrelated diversification, as plainly as it can be stated. In response to an interviewer's question — "Why do you believe so strongly in diversifying?" — Singleton's reply was:

> The principal reason is the natural desire of companies to survive. If you remain in one single line, you will not survive. Everything has its day. You can't wait to see what is going to replace what you are doing.
>
> Concurrent with the instinct for survival is the desire to grow. If you want to grow — the purpose being clearly to increase the company's strength and give it greater potential for survival — this can be accomplished by having a number of lines and phasing out the old ones as time goes by. I'm talking about the long term.[11]

Initially, size alone was the measure of success. The largest industrials were those viewed as the most efficient, profitable, and respected. Once a leadership position had been attained, a company did not easily yield it. Chief executives were expected to maintain or improve their industry position. Nor would they likely hold their office if a company's ranking was to suddenly drop.

In the dynamics of competition, companies continue to joust to improve their relative standings. Anticipating what competitors *might* do tempers the strategy of what companies actually do. And those with dominant market shares realize they have a prize others covet. Rather than waiting to be preempted, firms invest and actively expand in the desire to maintain market share and thus their competitive advantage, as well as anticipate the actions of others. Once in place, the managerial hierarchy becomes a principal motivator for continued growth and accumulation of power. This is as true today as it has been in the past and will be in the future. There is little doubt that growth is as powerful a force for today's professionally managed firms as it was for the owner-entrepreneurs of an earlier era.

The conglomerate phenomenon has been difficult to adequately comprehend because it is still ongoing. Currently the move to rationalize conglomerates is being blurred by leveraged buy-outs, takeovers by individual financiers, conglomerates buying other conglomerates, and broker-sponsored buy-outs and takeovers. All seem to belie any systematic single trend. But the future of conglomerates lies with the professionally managed firms that have adopted the strategy. Without this endorsement by the corporate establishment, the problems inherent in conglomeration might have prevented further evolution. Yet the move to rationalize, already in motion, will continue. Large companies in mature businesses will either diversify or become acquired. Since advances in management typically lag behind changes in strategy, it is the *management* of diversification that deserves the greatest attention now.

Notes

1. Hannah Leslie, "Mergers," in the *Encyclopedia of American Economic History: Studies of the Principal Movements and Ideas.* Ed. Glenn Porter. Volume II. New York: Charles Scribner's Sons, 1980, p. 643.
2. *Forbes,* January 1, 1963, p. 35.
3. Edith T. Penrose, *The Theory of the Growth of the Firm.* Oxford: Basil Blackwell, 1959, p. 40.
4. *Forbes,* January 1, 1963, p. 39.
5. "Interview of Royal Little," *Dun's Review,* May, 1968.
6. *Wall Street Journal,* March 7, 1975, p. 1.
7. *Forbes,* April 1, 1977, p. 48.
8. *Forbes,* January 9, 1978, p. 94, and *Forbes,* January 1, 1975, p. 178.
9. *Fortune,* February 1967, p. 131.
10. *Forbes,* January 1, 1976, p. 62.
11. *Forbes,* September 15, 1967, p. 230.

2 DEBUNKING
THE MYTHS

T HERE IS CONSIDERABLE TRUTH to some of the accusations made against conglomerates. Stories of inept or inexplicable behavior are common. Jimmy Ling, the founder of Ling-Temco-Vought (now LTV), was described by *Fortune* as a person who "had brought together — and sometimes took apart — many operating companies in a breathless series of purchases, mergers, and spin-offs, amid a profusion of offerings and exchanges of virtually every type of security known to investors."[1] Under Charles Bludhorn, Gulf & Western acquired a bewildering array of companies in a brief span of time with the connecting strategic links, if any, obvious only to Mr. Bludhorn. U.S. Industries acquired more than 100 small companies in one year and tried to operate each one as an autonomous business. Criticism of these and other instances of haphazard strategy is understandable.

But building a positive case for the general concept of conglomerates doesn't mean apologizing for the actions of specific companies. Poor execution isn't a monopoly of conglomerate firms. The indisputable fact is that from the middle of the 1950s an increasing number of companies have diversified, and continue to diversify, away from original lines of business. Since the conglomerate strategy already reflects the way many big businesses think — and the trend appears to be here to stay — we'd best try to begin to understand it. To do so, some of the more pervasive myths that surround conglomerates need to be dispelled first.

MYTH #1: CONGLOMERATE DIVERSIFICATION DOESN'T MAXIMIZE SHAREOWNERS' INTERESTS

A common dismissal of the conglomerate strategy of diversification is that it is unnecessary. Companies should reflect the interests of their shareowners, the argument goes, and if shareowners wish diversification they can do so individually by changing the mix of corporate shares held in their portfolio of investments. Managers would do better to stick to a specialization, and let their shareowners do the diversifying.

But this ready-made answer to unrelated diversification denies management's right to make decisions *on behalf of* its shareowners. Managers are obliged, as representatives of owners' interests, to make the best business judgments they can. They must use their managerial talents to determine the most appropriate strategies to follow, and with an increasing number of managers choosing unrelated diversification, they have demonstrated that, in their professional opinions, specialization is not always the better strategy.

The assumption that "shareowners must be served" has been carried over from the time when owners were managers. In mercantile days, the owner of a business ran it personally. Shareowners and managers views were the same. This identity of interests, however, has long been the exception rather than the rule for big business. As far back as 1932, Berle and Means's book, *The Modern Corporation,* clearly documented that owners no longer ran large businesses. Owners concluded that the complexities of business required professional management, so they gave up their managerial role in exchange for hired expertise. Managers, in turn, were expected to apply their skills at optimizing the company's performance, and thus *indirectly* maximize the owner's investment. Shareowners could still replace managements, but new managers would be hired who could also exercise their professional judgment.

Every strategy must rest on its merits. Whether specialization or diversification is the correct strategy for a particular company is only one of the many decisions that managements are entrusted to make for their shareowners. Individual shareowners who do not agree with a firm's policies are free to sell their shares and purchase stock in companies more to their liking. To suggest that because shareowners *can* diversify their investments managers somehow *shouldn't* is connecting two unrelated issues.

In fact, the proposition that managers should be rooted in a business could force them into pursuing patently "bad" management practices, for example, sticking with a declining or deteriorating market. Should managers risk joining the list of companies that couldn't adapt to change, or stay with dying industries until they are dragged down with them? As illustrated by the table on page 30, few of the major industrials operating in 1909 remain independent, and some have been liquidated altogether. While shareowners can easily sell their shares if they see disaster coming, are managers expected to go down with their corporate ship?

An endorsement of "shareowners' interests" also raises the question of which group of shareowners should be served, and to what purpose? Shareowners are not a homogeneous group with a single point of view. Individual shareowners are increasingly being joined by institutional owners; i.e., banks, insurance companies, and mutual funds. These institutions own over one-third of the voting stock of companies listed on the New York Stock Exchange. On a typical trading day on the exchange, up to 75 percent and more of the trading activity can be accounted for by institutions. Another type of "owner," especially where acquisitions are concerned, is the professional arbitrageur. Arbitrageurs will buy stock upon announcement of an impending merger in the hope that the final acquisition price will be bid higher than their entry cost. Finally, there are takeover specialists who pursue undervalued situations, not primarily to run the company but to make a financial gain from investing in its stock. Notorious raiders like Saul Steinberg, Carl Icahn, Victor Posner, and T. Boone Pickens, by threatening to take over companies, have negotiated very profitable buyouts from managements anxious to remain independent.

In a takeover, whose rights are managers to maximize? Individual shareowners generally look to immediate financial gain since they have no vested managerial or operating connections with a company. Institutional holders of shares have a responsibility to accept the most "attractive" purchase offers — placing them in a position of willing sellers instead of personally involved owners. Arbitrageurs are high-risk stock traders, in for the quick kill. Takeover artists like T. Boone Pickens, despite his championing of the rights of small shareholders, have obvious high personal stakes in the financial outcome of their investments. According to British raider Sir James Goldsmith, while a takeover may be for the public good, that's not why he does it. "I do it to make money," he says.

None of the above "owners" make their decisions from the perspective of an owner-manager, but rather from the financial orientation of an investor, and a quick profit is often preferred by investors to risking the workout of long-range strategies. All we know about sound strategic management

Disposition of the Fifty Largest Industrials in 1909
(ranked according to size of assets)

Company	No Longer Independent	Still Independent (Name change)
1. U.S. Steel		Same
2. Standard Oil of N.J.		(Exxon)
3. American Tobacco		(American Brands)
4. International Harvester		Same
5. Amalgamated Copper	Acquired by ARCO — 1977	
6. Central Leather	Liquidated — 1953	
7. Pullman	Acquired by Wheelabrator – Frye — 1980	
8. Armour	Acquired by General Host — 1969	
9. American Sugar		(Amstar — a private company)
10. U.S. Rubber		(Uniroyal)
11. American Smelting & Refining		(Asarco)
12. Singer Manufacturing		(Singer)
13. Swift	Fresh meat operations continue as an independent company	Swift International
14. Pittsburgh Coal	Acquired by Consolidated Coal — 1966	
15. General Electric		Same
16. American Car & Foundry		(ACF — a private company)
17. Colorado Fuel & Iron	Acquired by Crane — 1969	
18. Corn Products		(General Foods)
19. American Can		Same
20. Lackawanna	Acquired by Bethlehem Steel — 1923	
21. American Woolens	Acquired by Textron — 1955	
22. Westinghouse		Same
23. Consolidation Coal	Acquired by Continental Oil — 1967	
24. DuPont		Same
25. Republic Steel	Merged with LTV — 1984	(LTV Steel)
26. Va-Carolina Chemical	Acquired by Mobil — 1962	
27. International Paper		Same
28. Bethlehem Steel		Same
29. American Locomotive	Acquired by Worthington — 1964	
30. National Biscuit	Merged with Standard Brands — 1981	(Nabisco Brands)
31. Cambria Steel	Acquired by Midvale Steel — 1916	
32. Chile Copper*	Acquired by Anaconda — 1923	
33. Distillers Securities**		(National Distillers)
34. Calumet & Hecla	Acquired by UOP — 1968	

Disposition of the Fifty Largest Industrials in 1909
(ranked according to size of assets) (*Cont.*)

Company	No Longer Independent	Still Independent (Name change)
35. American Agricultural Chemical	Acquired by Continental Oil — 1963	
36. Allis-Chalmers		Same
37. Crucible Steel	Acquired by Colt Industry — 1968	
38. Lake Superior	Unknown end	
39. U.S. Smelting & Refining	In Liquidation — 1979	
40. United Copper	Liquidated — 1913	
41. National Lead		(NL Industries)
42. Phelps Dodge		Same
43. Lehigh Coal	Liquidated — 1965	
44. International Steam Pump	Liquidated — 1915	
45. Jones & Laughlin	Acquired by LTV — 1974	
46. Western Electric	Part of AT&T	
47. Associated Oil**	Acquired by Tidewater Assoc. Oil — 1926	
48. Am. Writing Paper	Liquidated — 1962	
49. Copper Range	Unknown end	
50. United Fruit	Merged into AMK — 1970	(United Brands)

* Chandler's listing included only 49 firms. Chile Copper was assumed to be the missing 32nd largest industrial.

** Both companies listed as number 33 by Chandler.

Source: Listing of firms based on Chandler, Alfred D., Jr., "The Beginnings of 'Big Business' in American Industry," *Business History Review,* Spring, 1959, Table 1. Dispositions are by the author.

of business, on the other hand, stresses the building of long-term operating excellence in companies. Surely, the short term and purely financial orientation of the average shareowner is not always the best way to manage American business. A preoccupation with such short-term financial decision-making has led to neglect of long-term investments in the production and operations side of American business, and a lessened ability to compete with such tough competitors as the Japanese, according to some authorities.

In sum, the argument of shareowners' interests to show that unrelated diversification is unwarranted is not a terribly solid one. Questions about how managers *should* behave in particular situations, such as during unfriendly acquisitions and takeovers, and whether a long-term or short-term view of management is appropriate, remain legitimate subjects for debate. A clarification of these duties, however, is not helped by stating that managers must "serve the interests of shareowners."

MYTH #2: INVESTMENT DECISIONS
SHOULD BE MADE BY THE CAPITAL MARKETS

Another oversimplification used against conglomerates is the assumption of perfect capital markets. The same persons who advance the notion of shareowners' interests suggest that corporations' investments should be subject to the willingness of the markets to provide financing. Regardless of any theoretical benefits, this is not, in fact, how managers act. Based on a limited sample of successful, mature companies, two leading Harvard professors conducted a careful and thorough study of the financial and psychological forces that shaped top managers' strategic choices, and concluded that: "Those who argue that management strives to maximize shareholder wealth have also argued that management's strategic decisions are subject to the discipline of the capital market. From their perspective management's choices are guided by the corporate rate of return on investment compared to the cost of that capital in the public markets. But we have found that the top managers in these large, mature companies seek to *minimize* their dependence on the external capital markets."[2]

Company executives apparently do not care to subject themselves to the market's discipline or conflicting investors' objectives and expectations. Consequently companies strive first to fund projects from internal sources, and in many instances, while the "capital market window may never be literally closed, for practical purposes it remains shut because these managers are unwilling to step up to it." Simply put, a lesson managers gained from experience was that "the only truly loyal money was money over which they had direct control."[3]

This insight helps explain why companies seek unrelated diversification. Within an organization of different businesses, the alternative uses for capital are greater. By remaining concentrated in one industry, on the other hand, capital allocation tends to be reinvested in that industry. For a company with a significant market share in a mature industry, chances are that it is generating more cash than it can profitably reinvest — the proverbial cash cow. From this point, it can either give surplus cash flows back to the shareholders, reduce its capitalization, or diversify. Managers haven't been overly disposed to the first alternative and the second is not a solution that can be pursued indefinitely. This leaves diversification as a viable option for companies oriented toward maintaining their historic rate of growth.

In effect, an internal capital market exists in every company made up of the cash flows it generates. These monies are employed at the discretion of management and, in the case of conglomerates, may be used to fund new businesses that will help the corporation grow and prosper. This is the essence of the motivation behind unrelated acquisitions. Royal Little, the founder of Textron, provides a good illustration of this conglomerate logic in describing the acquisition of Homelite.

> You had to find companies that had the potential, even if they were very small, to increase earnings either by growing or by reducing costs. When we bought a chainsaw company called Homelite Corp. in 1955, it was tiny compared with its competitor, McCulloch Corp. But we knew McCulloch had a high-cost operation beside the Los Angeles airport. So we moved Homelite out of unionized New England and built beautiful new plants down South, and we beat McCulloch with lower costs. . . . Homelite sales, along with those of two small metal fastener companies we acquired in the 1950s, Townsend Co. and Camcar Manufacturing Co., are now more than ten times what they were when we bought them.[4]

MYTH #3: CONGLOMERATES DON'T PROVIDE ECONOMIC BENEFITS

An objective analysis of conglomerates has also been handicapped by prevailing economic theory. Over the years, the justification for diversification has been anchored to the notion of lowering *costs*. The more companies are alike, the more costs they can eliminate by combining. A merger of two competitors, for example, would produce cost savings by eliminating duplicate or overlapping functions of advertising, sales, distribution, and general and administrative expenses. At the other extreme is the completely unrelated merger, such as an auto-parts distributor acquiring a finance company. Here there are no apparent cost reductions from merging common activities.

As logical as the above argument may appear, it has limitations. For one thing, its origins go back roughly two hundred years to the writings of Adam Smith. Adam Smith showed that costs decline when production is broken into specialized tasks. Because large scale businesses permit greater specialization of production, greater cost savings are achievable. And as long as companies remain committed to an industry, ever greater familiarity and specialization of routine tasks will continue to promote economic efficiency.

There is nothing wrong with Adam Smith's logic, but a lot of things have changed since his day. Companies have moved beyond a one-industry concentration. As old businesses matured, firms began looking for new growth opportunities. Conglomerates in particular developed a strategy based on the pursuit of higher sales and profits as a motivation for changing industries. Instead of seeking solely to reduce costs, they also tried to increase sales and profits by diversifying into potentially more attractive and faster growing businesses. Lord John Maynard Keynes once observed that "the engine which drives enterprise is not thrift but profit." One of the reasons that economists have resisted Keynes's insight is because it clashes with well-established principles of synergy that rest on lower costs and relatedness of operations.

Recently, a new theory has appeared from the field of industrial economics that recognizes the possibility, and even the desirability, of companies freely crossing industry boundaries. Under this new concept of "contestable markets," companies should be free to seek opportunity wherever it might appear.[5] Pockets of inefficiency that exist in unrelated industries represent opportunities for those firms equipped to grasp them, and such opportunities *should* be "contested" for by companies outside as well as inside the industry.

The crux of this new theory is freedom of market entry and exit. Once companies are no longer assumed to be tied to an industry — because of the advantages of industry specialization — conglomerate-style diversification becomes possible in theory as well as practice. In fact, diversification is accepted as almost inevitable in *perfectly* contestable industries — those where there is complete freedom to enter and exit. In a broader vein, companies with distinctive competence may be *driven* to operate in unrelated industries if they can maximize profits by doing so.

MYTH #4: RELATEDNESS IS A BETTER STRATEGY

Even if companies diversify, they should not stray far from the business they are in. This message is basically the one conveyed by Peters and Waterman in their book *In Search of Excellence,* and it is consistent with most economists' argument of sticking to an area of specialization.

Peters and Waterman go out of their way to argue *against* conglomerates as a way to build their case *for* relatedness. This is unfortunate, because the positive messages in their book are very instructive. For instance, the authors see distinctive competences, or "core skills," as they put it, as the basis for successful diversification. Yet Peters and Waterman seem to have a very narrow view of diversification. They do not see the dangers of staying too long in a business where, despite the fact that management has good core skills, the core itself is rotting.

If *In Search of Excellence* had been written twenty years ago, the Mesta Machine Company might have been one of the companies chosen to be in the select group of excellently managed firms. It qualified as a recognized leader in its field. Its plants, like Dana's — one of the "excellent" companies identified by Peters and Waterman — made products for the mature steel industry. Like Dana, it specialized in an unenticing array of products, including steel-mill machinery, ship-propeller shafts, and giant turbines. And like Dana, top management concentrated on a few things and did them very well. Moreover, communications with its employees was a trademark of Mesta's human relations policy. A worker in the machine shop since 1933 commented on the chief executive of Mesta: "He really knew how to instill pride. We had then what the Japanese are talking about now."

In short, Dana and the former Mesta Machine Company shared many attributes. Both were considered excellently managed companies in their prime, emphasized face-to-face communications, enjoyed good profitability, and served mature markets. Unfortunately, Mesta landed in Chapter 11 of the Federal Bankruptcy Code on February 9, 1983. A chronicle of its ills covers a host of common pressures: foreign competitors, outmoded technology, and escalating costs. But the one overriding factor was its inability to recognize the need for change. When the steel industry began its decline, Mesta was pulled in its wake. Of course, Mesta may not have avoided bankruptcy regardless of what it did. But by remaining devoted to an aging and technologically backward industry, it practically sealed its fate.

By stretching a good idea beyond its limits, Peters and Waterman dilute the positive case they make for operating efficiently *within* a particular market. Their approach denies the possibility of excellence by diversifying much beyond that market. But even as they were writing, evolutionary pressures were making many of their arguments obsolete. For example, General Motors diversified into the computer business by acquiring Electronic Data Systems (EDS). By this one move, GM violated three of Peters and Waterman's guidelines for excellence: stay close to your industry, have intimate knowledge of the business you're buying, and buy small so you can assimilate the newcomer. Does this mean GM's strategy is faulty? Neither Peters and Waterman nor anyone else can say for sure. What it appears to demonstrate is a conclusion reached by General Motors, U.S. Steel, and other large companies in mature industries. That is, the outcome of staying with a maturing and fiercely competitive business is risky and relatively predictable. In comparison, diversification poses risks of another sort — but also the possibility for better overall performance.

The intent here is not to imply that Dana will share Mesta's fate, or that GM or U.S. Steel can excel by diversifying, but to underline the fallacy of mistaking excellence in running a business for good overall strategy in managing a corporation. One of the executives in a company surveyed by Peters and Waterman proudly exclaimed: "Never acquire a business you don't know how to manage." That's a good thought — as far as it goes. But a corollary comment might be, "Avoid staying in a business simply because you're comfortable running it."

A variation on the claim that relatedness is a better strategy has been to diffuse the idea of relatedness so that diversification into *entirely different businesses* can still be construed as "related diversification." Every company shares common functions like marketing, production, technology, accounting, and sales. This fact of similarity can be stretched — depending on who's making the determination — to qualify any combination as "related" and thus avoid dealing with conglomerates as a separate species of corporation altogether.

The potential for confusion here is demonstrated by a personal experience. In addressing a seminar of Ph.D. students at a leading university recently, I made a passing reference to United Technologies, a very large conglomerate. A hand shot up immediately. United Technologies is not a conglomerate because it only participates in businesses "technologically related" to one another, one of the students claimed. Pushed to explain the compatibility, technological or otherwise, between air conditioners, computers, elevators, and jet engines, the student insisted these were all "technologically oriented" businesses. Does this mean, I persisted, that because Buicks and bicycles both use ball bearings that such commonality excuses all their differences? Presuming I had missed his point, the student merely smiled.

Departing from the accepted measure of diversification according to participation in different businesses — the criterion used by *Fortune, Forbes,* the Federal Trade Commission, the Securities and Exchange Commission, and most researchers — invites confusion. Is Coca-Cola's purchase of Columbia Industries motion-picture business a "related acquisition" because Coca-Cola is sold in movie theatres? This may seem like a frivolous example, but it is by no means an impossible interpretation, once sufficient latitude is given in defining related diversification.

MYTH #5: CONGLOMERATES CAN'T BE MANAGED

The claim that conglomerates are unmanageable has a familiar ring. The same charge was made when giant firms were created in the early 1900s. A similar line of reasoning was used. Large organizations strain the capacity of top management to control them. As the number of departments and people multiply, the complexity of managing increases. At some point, the system becomes overloaded. The centralized control network will be too weak to meet the mushrooming demands on it. This limitation has even been stated mathematically, with optimum size considered the point just before the advantages of scale are outweighed by the costs of administration.

This principle of diminishing returns to increasing size is true only if administrative capabilities remain frozen. Assuming no changes, controls would break down. As for the managerial inefficiencies of conglomerates, it is a matter of carrying this line of reasoning to an extreme. If size alone is a problem, the new complexity of the conglomerate form poses truly formidable odds. Control is complicated by the variety of specializations, products, markets, and cultures.

But companies must change in order to pursue better strategies. And administrative systems have adjusted in order to accomodate new strategies. To handle greater size, for example, companies adopted new organizational designs, moving from a functional structure for a single industry orientation to a multidivisional structure as companies moved into related business lines. Such administrative adaptation did not convert every skeptic. However, the unmanageability thesis became increasingly hard to defend as big companies continued to grow even bigger. In 1959, an economist studying the theory of the growth of firms made the following remark on the assumed limits of size:

". . . The question of whether firms can get 'too big' for efficiency is the wrong question, for there is no reason to assume that as the large firms grow larger they will become inefficient; it is much more likely that their organization will become so different that we must look on them differently. We cannot define a caterpillar and then use the same definition for a butterfly."[6]

Past flexibility in administration has permitted large integrated firms to be managed efficiently. With appropriate innovations, conglomerates can also master the art of managing. Administrative adaptibility is, in fact, a necessary step in unlocking the potential for a conglomerate strategy that has already arrived. It does not mean that every multibusiness firm will manage its complexity successfully. It does, however, suggest that the large numbers of very diversified companies that have survived will develop administrative systems that can handle the new strategy.

A major breakthrough in dealing with diversification has been the computer. Computerized information systems are to complexity what railroads and telegraphy were to volume expansion. For conglomerates, widespread diversification couldn't possibly be handled without the computer. Computer-based management information systems are essential for keeping top managers informed on operations in a decentralized, multibusiness firm. Computers do not guarantee effective management, of course. And computers may never fulfill the inflated claims that announced their arrival. However, they are highly efficient filing systems for storing and sorting large amounts of data. Had the computer permitted nothing more than the consolidation of budgets and plans among various businesses, it would have made a major contribution to decentralized management.

Other administrative innovations will be needed to advance the art of conglomerate management — with some possibilities discussed in a later chapter. Looking back on the current administrative problem of conglomerates years from now, their degree of complexity will probably seem tame.

MYTH #6: CONGLOMERATES ARE POOR PERFORMERS

Another argument used against conglomerates is based on statistical studies of performance. If conglomerates represent a superior strategy, then their performance record should be superior. This cause-and-effect relationship is unconfirmed in a number of statistical tests on the effects of diversification.

Quantitative testing in general is supposed to demonstrate the validity of a hypothesis of how things should be. But in periods of transition, like the current restructuring of American industry, statistical measures alone cannot objectively sort out all the changes that are taking place. Many, many static pictures over time are needed to portray an entire evolutionary cycle. Trying to explain dynamic change, as in the case of conglomerates, by a single snapshot of the past is like trying to negotiate a curve in the road by looking in the rearview mirror.

As a matter of principle, unequivocal findings of good or bad performance under changing conditions would be unusual. Researchers may and often do see the unexplained portion of their data according to whether or not they agree with the prevailing wisdom. In developing formulas to explain evolutionary changes, what researchers tend to confirm is what they went in believing.

Royal Little, the founder of Textron and one of the fathers of the modern conglomerate, unsurprisingly found much to admire about conglomerates in an article appropriately titled "Conglomerates Are Doing Better Than You Think."[7] His findings are contrary to a number of academic studies with conflicting — but equally predictable — conclusions. Without taking sides, a middle ground is probable. Sometimes conglomerates perform better; sometimes they don't. Performances by a large sample of companies based on standard financial measures is available from data compiled by *Forbes* since 1963. Comparing conglomerates* to all industries according to compounded rates of growth in sales and earnings and return on equity and return on total capital, the following figure shows that conglomerates tend to look good in some measures during some periods and underperform at other times. The record is not consistent. That shouldn't come as any surprise. The claim made for conglomerates is not that theirs is a perfect or superior strategy, merely a lasting one. The fact that the universe of conglomerates includes some "bad" performers should be expected in any sample of companies in an emergent stage of development.

The reality is that mismanagement and poor performance are found in undiversified and diversified companies alike. A number of companies made strategic faux pas by staying with industries like leather, coal, and steel. Major realignments among leading industries also have toppled once dominant companies. Conglomerates remind us that change remains a constant. When evaluating data that suggest otherwise, it is good to

---

*Over the years, a number of definitions of *conglomerate* have been used. In this figure, the *most* diversified type of company has consistently been chosen as the basis for the comparisons.

Typical Annual Planning Cycle

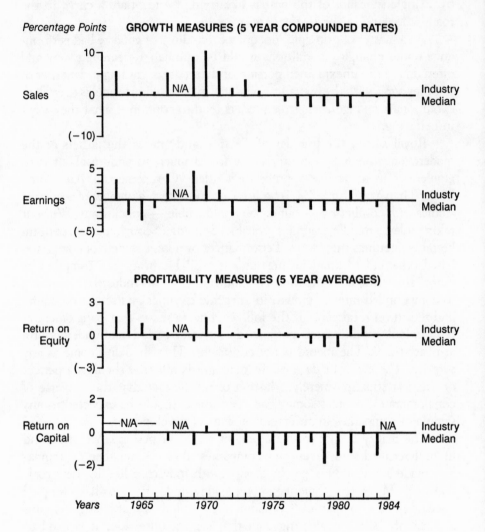

Percentage Points   **GROWTH MEASURES (5 YEAR COMPOUNDED RATES)**

Sales   Industry
                                                                                         Median

Earnings   Industry
                                                                                         Median

PROFITABILITY MEASURES (5 YEAR AVERAGES)

Return on   Industry
Equity   Median

Return on   Industry
Capital   Median

Years   1965   1970   1975   1980   1984

keep one eye open on the observable, measurable contradictions that surround us.

MYTH #7: CONGLOMERATES PROMOTE "PAPER ENTREPRENEURIALISM"

Conglomerates misallocate resources, it is claimed, by practicing a form of "paper entrepreneurialism," whereby pieces of paper are exchanged for corporate assets, with no new productive capacity to show for it.

This argument either misses the point of diversification, or is deliberately misleading. Like any company, a conglomerate will try to maximize returns. If this can be better accomplished by buying existing assets rather than building them, it would be an uneconomic and wasteful use of resources to do otherwise. Whether the assets purchased prove to be productive or not will be judged by others. Success or failure in conglomerate and non-conglomerate acquisitions alike is reflected in overall performance. Unwise moves that drag down total performance create inefficiencies that attract new acquirors. In effect, the market for investments is self-correcting, with many investors always on the lookout for situations that appear undervalued. This scrutiny for underperformers should motivate conglomerate managers always to stress operating improvements in a business after it is purchased, or suffer the consequences.

In the early to mid-1980s, divestitures of divisions that failed to realize their expected potential, and even takeover and dismemberment of some conglomerates themselves, were the price paid for failing to operate efficiently. In the 1970s, large numbers of haphazard acquisitions made a decade or so earlier were divested. Conglomerates found that unsound acquisitions, which could be carried for a time by a booming economy, became eventual liabilities.

In an open marketplace, the perpetual search for undervalued situations keeps managers striving to maximize returns in order to avoid bids by acquirors that believe they can improve another firm's performance. Such checks and countermoves by companies are part of a dynamic capital market. Attempts to outmaneuver competitors are an inherent part of the system. Occasionally, it is true, rules can be twisted to unfair advantage for one side or the other. In 1970, for instance, Opinion 17 issued by the Accounting Standards Board revised the use of "pooling of interests" account-

Controversial Takeover Tactics

Greenmailing

A practice that involves a two-stage strategy of first buying a minority interest in a business, and then negotiating with management to buy back that position at an above-market price. An especially successful maneuver of this type was conducted by Saul Steinberg when Walt Disney bought back his 11 percent share in the company at a price $12 above what other shareholders could get for their stock at the time. This earned Steinberg a quick $59 million. Even more successful was the Bass brothers' green-mailing of Texaco. They reaped $280 million in just forty-nine days for buying under 10 percent of Texaco's stock. In effect, greenmail is the price companies are willing to pay in return for the derailment of a possible unfriendly takeover.

Golden Parachutes

Top executives may provide lucrative compensation for themselves in the case of a takeover. These normally very generous packages are referred to as *golden parachutes*. The classic parachute was Bill Agee's $5.4 million severance arrangement triggered when Bendix was acquired by Allied Corporation. According to one report, more than 60 percent of the top executives of the 1,000 largest firms had such golden parachutes by the end of 1982.

Poison Pills

In order to avoid being taken over, a company can take a number of actions that will make it a less desirable target. This may involve selling a profitable division, issuing extra shares, or acquiring other companies. Textron, for example, was rumored to have bought Avco, a very diversified manufacturer, in order to repel unfriendly takeovers. The ensuing increase in debt to finance the acquisition, along with the sheer size and complexity of the combination, was expected to persuade takeover artists to look elsewhere.

ing. Pooling had afforded companies wide latitude in how earnings could be calculated and led to exaggerated performance measures by some conglomerates. Today some of the takeover practices also involve legal but increasingly questionable tactics, such as "greenmailing," "poison pills," and "golden parachutes." (See the box.)

Assuming a level playing field, however, the best competitors will prevail. With freedom of competition, consumer welfare is enhanced. Without conglomerate-style entry, moreover, industries would become insulated and the level of competition influenced by a few leading firms in each major industry. Complacency and inefficiency would be protected within such environments. Indeed, only by external entry and the threat of new competitors are companies motivated to remain innovative and efficient.

Achieving greater efficiency and overall consumer welfare can, however, cause short-term disruptions. Major changes may adversely affect companies that have not adapted. The development of jet propulsion harmed companies that stuck with propeller-driven aircraft engines. Invention of color television helped RCA but injured competitors who bet on a permanent black-and-white picture. Deregulation of trucking, railroading, and airlines is causing dislocations in these industries. Acquisition of an inefficiently run business may lead to closing of outmoded facilities or replacement of old technologies, and these actions can have trickle-down repercussions among unions, suppliers, and communities. Each interest group will try to protect itself. That is natural and expected. But to the extent that such policies overrule the legitimate pursuit of more efficient operations, they work to the detriment of the general consumer welfare and erode the nation's competitive strength.

In sum, "paper entrepreneurialism" is a false issue that has no special application for conglomerates. Buying rather than building capacity is a common strategy among many companies, whether they acquire competitors, businesses in closely related lines, or totally unrelated firms. Those who decry "paper entrepreneurialism" use conglomerates as a diversion for a fundamentally different view of how the nation's resources *should* be allocated. The specifics of "paper entrepreneurialism" generally come down to a proposal for centralized planning, guided by a few master planners. It is an idea that is periodically introduced in one form or another. While not bluntly stated, the implication is clear that businessmen and investors alone can't be trusted with running the business of America. In lieu of the impartial decisions of the capital market, an elite few would assure the greater welfare of us all. Resources would be allocated more efficiently, because the planners in the know would be in charge. The poor record of attempts to control investment does not diminish the ardor of those who itch to try. In final analysis, theirs is an argument of politics rather than economics.

MYTH #8: CONGLOMERATES EXERT TOO MUCH ECONOMIC CONTROL

Big business, and now big conglomerate business, has traditionally faced the populist distrust of concentrated power. Bigness implies economic power and large diversified enterprises exaggerate that potential. If the concentration of power argument could be conclusively demonstrated, then the case against conglomerates would be strengthened. So far, however, the debate has attracted many contestants but no unanimous decision. Whatever one's persuasion, a number of sophisticated studies can be marshalled in support.

Viewed alone, the conglomerate movement seems impressive. Viewed alongside the growth in influence by federal and state governments, labor unions, consumer groups, and other institutions not generally sympathetic to them, the relative position of conglomerates is at best unclear. Conglomerates are merely one of the visible hands trying to gain economic power. At the same time a number of other visible and often more influential hands serve to keep undue concentration of corporate power, including conglomerates, in check.

A point worth underlining about conglomerates is that while their formation is often dramatic and attracts considerable attention, the story of business has historically included comparable or greater growth by small firms. Increasing complexity and diversity create demands for specialized relationships with smaller firms. In terms of sheer numbers, small firms outmultiply large ones several times over. Comparing 1929 with 1971, one study revealed that assets of the 200 largest firms "grew about in step with that of all other corporations, say, by doubling, or something more. But the *number* of all other corporations grew by such a factor that 'the 200' of 1971 were now surrounded by almost five times as many, and considerably smaller, corporations as had been 'the 200' of 1929."[8] Thus, conglomerates are not growing by displacing small firms. Both coexist by drawing on each other, and the implication of crowding out is no more true now than it was fifty or a hundred years ago.

Another well-kept finding is the effect of conglomerate restructuring on increasing the numbers of entrepreneurially run small and medium-sized businesses. In almost any issue of the *Wall Street Journal* there appears at least one article about a conglomerate selling a division to its managers, spinning off an operation to function independently, or helping a unit complete a leveraged buyout. Some of these create fairly sizable new businesses, such as SeaLand, distributed to the shareholders of R.J. Reynolds Industries, its former parent, and which now operates as one of the largest independent ocean-transportation companies. Harley-Davidson also was sold to its managers by its parent, AMF, and now represents the only American toehold in the domestic motorcycle market. A vastly greater number of deals involves smaller businesses, creating a new legion of entrepreneurs and entrepreneurially run small firms. Having worked for big corporations, these entrepreneurs chose the freedom and challenge of running their own operation, as well as the opportunity to reap extraordinary personal rewards. And they are willing to undertake the high risks associated with the financial terms under which most such deals are made.

This dynamic new dimension of entrepreneurship is attributable directly to conglomerate-style diversification. By increasing industry competition, every company now must try and maximize the efficiency of operations, or risk attracting an acquiror's attention. This frequently results in selling units that companies no longer feel they can efficiently operate. The reasons are numerous. Small units may not justify the time and effort of big companies to run them. Overhead costs in a complex organization may be significantly higher than if a business were to be run independently. Some units no longer fit the parent's primary strategic thrust. Whatever the reasons, the outcome is impressive. Today, a new entrepreneurial class of owner/managers has emerged, one that couldn't have been possible without the competitive stimulus of the conglomerate movement. Such restructuring of the second and third tiers of business is a potent weapon for reviving the entrepreneurial spirit and innovation necessary to move our capitalistic society forward, a missing ingredient according to Joseph Schumpeter's pessimistic long-term view of capitalism.

Finally, the question of power is relative. Are there countervailing powers? Are there countervailing benefits? Almost no serious research of either topic has been undertaken, even though answers are critical to a proper overall evaluation of conglomerates.

For example, global competition for large diversified U.S. firms is a fact of life. The substantive question then becomes how "powerful" are U.S. firms relative to their foreign counterparts. As a general response, a casual review of the evidence reveals that the growth rate of the top 100 foreign firms has far outstripped that of the top 100 U.S. firms. By 1977, the assets of the former exceeded those of the latter by over ten percent, and they have been gaining since.

The trend to greater diversification has tended to be emulated by these large foreign adversaries. In many cases, mergers are encouraged or tolerated as a means of gaining on large diversified U.S. corporations. Also, in diversified companies, cash flows from other businesses can be diverted in order to nurture new businesses or new technologies through the difficult start-up period in foreign markets. In penetrating our domestic automobile, motorcycle, electronic, video and television markets, some of the most aggressive and successful strategies were those of large diversified Japanese companies.

In Japan, government policy may actively encourage selected types of diversification. Honda, Mitsubishi, Matsushita, Nissan, or Hitachi need no lessons in diversification from U.S. conglomerates. Moreover, these are precisely the companies that are moving up in the world rankings, in many cases ahead of their American counterparts. A sobering statistic to contemplate is that in 1967 only one Japanese firm barely made the list of the world's fifty largest industrials. In 1983, there were five in the top fifty.

Documentation on the industrial development of foreign businesses is not as extensive as our own. What the available literature suggests, however, is a pattern that imitates the evolutionary progress of U.S. business, but lags behind. This allowed American corporations a comfortable margin after World War II, when most foreign competitors had to rebuild. That source of comfort is quickly vanishing, however. If large foreign conglomerates seize the initiative and outperform their U.S. competitors, the internal debate over distribution of power among the nation's corporations will be rendered moot. Can we risk sticking with an ideological argument that in the end proves hollow? If size and diversity spell competitive advantage, it is not a discovery that will do us much good if foreign competitors are allowed to exploit such an advantage first.

Notes

1. *Fortune*, January 1967, p. 137.
2. Gordon Donaldson and Jay W. Lorsch, *Decision Making at the Top*. New York: Basic Books, 1983, p. 7.
3. Ibid., pp. 52 and 166.
4. *Fortune*, May 28, 1984, p. 52.
5. William J. Baumol, John C. Panzai, and Robert D. Willig, *Contestable Markets and the Theory of Industry Structure*. New York: Harcourt Brace Jovanovich, 1982.
6. Edith T. Penrose, *The Theory of the Growth of the Firm*. Oxford: Basil Blackwell, 1959, p. 19.
7. *Fortune*, May 28, 1984, pp. 50 – 60.
8. John D. Glover, *The Evolutionary Corporations: Engines of Plenty, Engines of Growth, Engines of Change*. Homewood, Ill.: Dow Jones – Irwin, 1980, pp. 315 – 16.

3 CREATING VALUE IN THE CONGLOMERATE

T
HE WAY CONGLOMERATES can create value, or synergy, from combining unlike businesses has eluded both those who study them and those who manage them. Even among practitioners, one is hard pressed to find an articulate explanation of why conglomerates work. From a purely analytical point of view, unexplained actions are always suspect. On a practical level, an inability to describe the elements of strategy assures a long period of trial and error before a successful procedure is learned.

In fact, some lessons have already been learned. The first conglomerate entrepreneurs struck out into uncharted territory. Unrestricted by past assumptions about what they were attempting, they constructed large rambling enterprises, and left to their successors the job of making sense of the various pieces and effectively managing the whole. These were men guided by instinct rather than design. Short-term earnings projections from combining Company A with Company B often were justification enough. Synergy was no more sophisticated than the belief that two plus two would somehow equal five.

With the endorsement of the conglomerate concept by old-line industrial firms came the trappings of professional management. All the tools of systematic management are now available to rationalize what the early conglomerate entrepreneurs had envisioned. New tools of analysis also are available, like Strategic Business Units (SBU), Profit Impact of Market Strategies (PIMS), and the Boston Consulting Group's ubiquitous portfolio management matrix. New ways of competing within industries and among like competitors, has become a preoccupation with both managers and theorists. Books like Peters and Waterman's *In Search of Excellence* and Michael Porter's *Competitive Strategy* find receptive and wide audiences by stressing the virtues of relatedness and business-level strategy.

In the meantime, the strategic emphasis has shifted towards the corporate level. Only at the top is the view of the organization total, and only top managers can make decisions that alter the mix of businesses. Tactical or operations-based managing alone no longer suffices. The conglomerate, in sum, cries out for new conventional wisdom. It requires openness to the possibility of greater corporate effectiveness through change, in addition to maintaining efficient operations in present businesses (see the following diagram). Experts and managers are relying on old routes leading to past successes even while companies move in new directions that make them less applicable.

What creates value? What is the basis for forming effective strategic groups of businesses? Such questions of value creation, or *synergy*, remain unanswered. In this chapter, three means for obtaining synergy from unrelated acquisitions are proposed, from the easiest but least potent type — financial synergy — to the most difficult, but potentially rewarding, move of restructuring and integrating the acquired businesses.

FINANCIAL SYNERGY

There are two ways to make profits through unrelated acquisitions: better business management or better cash management. Financial synergy refers to the latter. No direct management of the business is required. Stated simply, it is a question of putting money to work wherever it can get the best return. Because companies tend to reinvest only in businesses they control, the mix of businesses become an issue in calculating returns of investment. If a steel company is tied to that industry, its investment decisions tend to be steel-related. If a company operates a steel business as well as a number of other businesses, as did Allegheny International, then the investment possibilities multiply. Ultimately investment decisions may even exclude steel because of an inferior rate of return, a decision Allegheny International implicitly made when it divested itself of Allegheny Ludlom Steel.

The financial approach is the easiest type of beginning acquisition for an aspiring conglomerate. It can be likened to a holding company arrangement common among utility companies in the 1930s where the parent did

A Comparative View of Planning for Effectiveness Versus Efficiency

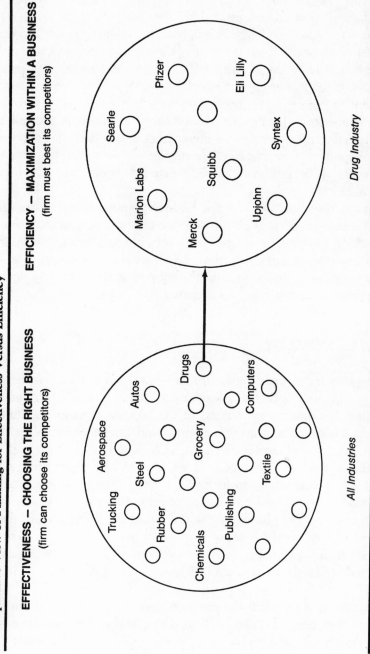

not directly involve itself in the affairs of its constituents. It was a style that suited the early conglomerate entrepreneurs, who were motivated to build vast empires quickly, with little thought to how they would be managed. They made acquisitions based on financial calculations that showed that the combined operations would increase earnings per share.

Complementary Cash Flows

The preferred approach for a company seeking financial synergy is to create a mix of businesses with complementary or offsetting industry characteristics. The better the match-up between financial strengths and weaknesses of individual parts, the greater the level of potential synergy for the corporation as a whole.

The most common vehicle for visualizing how financial synergy might work is the Boston Consulting Group's portfolio matrix of cows, stars, speculative ventures, and dogs, as illustrated in the following chart. The

Portfolio Matrix

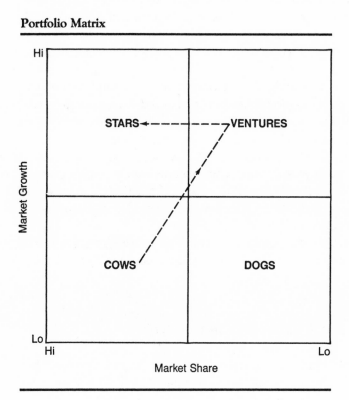

diagram displays the direction of cash flows. The excess cash generated by the cows would go to finance promising speculative ventures. The successful ventures would become stars, which, as their market matures, would generate excess cash in order to finance new speculative ventures. Norton, a diversified manufacturer, has employed the portfolio management system "as the heart of its total strategic planning process." In a traditional fashion, parts of the company were evaluated according to the quadrant of the matrix they occupied. Stars and selected ventures warranted most of the new investment monies, while cows and cash realized from sale of dogs provided the internal funds for the overall strategy.

For companies with a single large cash cow, the search for suitable stars or speculative ventures becomes urgent. Tobacco firms are a case in point. With unit growth in the domestic cigarette business growing slowly or declining, and health hazards a threat to the future of the industry, diversification into other businesses was a natural course to follow. For American Brands this meant widespread diversification into such areas as office products, cosmetics, food, liquor, life insurance, and protective services. R.J. Reynolds Tobacco changed its name to R.J. Reynolds Industries after moving into energy, ocean transportation, and food and beverages.

In 1983, Reynolds bought Heublein, itself a diversified food and beverage company. A need for cash was a major reason Heublein was available. It had diversified into fields it could not adequately finance to achieve their potential. Reynolds, on the other hand, is a large money machine. Cash flows from its cigarette business far exceed reinvestment needs. Also, Reynolds already was well along on a $1 billion modernization program in this core business. Del Monte, its other major food acquisition, had also been substantially modernized. Finally, Reynolds was considering disposal of its ocean transportation and energy businesses to concentrate on consumer goods, including food and beverages. Thus it was a marriage of dowry and promise. Equally compelling pressures of burgeoning cash flows and maturity or cyclicality in their core businesses have prompted companies like Burlington Northern, Goodyear, and Ryder Transportation to look for acquisitions complementing them in a financial sense but operating in different fields.

Don't Put All Your Eggs In One Basket

A second reason companies may seek to acquire unrelated businesses is to minimize the risks associated with putting all their assets in one industry. The chief executive officer of Kaman, for instance, vows never again to make his company vulnerable to a shutdown of the helicopter business as happened in 1966 when Kaman was a single-product firm. Having since diversified into three completely different markets of helicopters, musical instruments, and industrial distribution, the chief executive prefers this unlikely combination to the high risks of the cyclical single-product strategy.

Cooper Industries' top executive shares this philosophy. Operating a company involved with compressors, drilling equipment, hand tools, and electrical equipment, he now sacrifices profit surges for risk-spreading. "Finding a purely countercyclical business is wishful thinking," he believes. "What you try to do is get a variety of cycles going so that only rarely will they hit you all at once."

Another believer in spreading risk is American Standard, the largest plumbing supply manufacturer, a manufacturer of transportation equipment and most recently the acquiror of Trane, a maker of air conditioners. The Trane acquisition was expected to bolster American Standard's position in building products by supplying different ends of the spectrum. American Standard's sales are two-thirds residential with a large international sales component, while Trane's products are mainly custom built for commercial and industrial buildings, mostly in the United States. Thus while one part of the building market may be in a slump, there now is an ability to compensate by maintaining sales at the other end.

Banking on the Future

A third financial strategy is for larger, well-resourced companies to acquire equity positions in emerging new technology firms. In exotic technologies like biotechnology and robotics, the negative cash flows can last for many years and tax the resources and capability of small firms to go it alone.

The explosion of the new field of biotechnology, for instance, holds more promise than the many new companies can finance themselves. Accordingly a number of large companies have purchased equity interests in the hopes of garnering a stake in one of the winners in this technological race. Of the more than 100 gene-splicing firms, a few are leading the pack and all of these have large corporate shareowners. These investors include American Cynamid, Standard Oil of Indiana, Standard Oil of California, Martin Marietta, Lubrizol, Monsanto, Koppers, and National Distillers and Chemicals. This heterogeneous group shares a desire to ride this new technology into a significant new business opportunity.

In one of the more bizarre examples of old and new, France's major cement maker, Lafarge Copée, acquired a $160 million stake in a biotechnology firm making amino acids for feed supplements and pharmaceuticals. Not a textbook case of diversification, perhaps, but one with an underlying explanation. Being the world's third largest cement manufacturer, Lafarge Copée was resigned to a modest 1 percent to 2 percent annual growth in their original business. "We want to be the best, if not necessarily the biggest, cement maker in the world," said the CEO of Lafarge Copée. "But," he added, "there is no high growth future in cement." Thus, the company had little choice but to diversify if it was to meet its two-tiered objective of high growth and the reduction of cement to less than half of the company's profit in twenty years.

Not all new ventures require the help of a bigger company. Some promising new firms are self-financed or backed by venture capitalists and do not seek a corporate partner. In key industries like semiconductors, however, the large group of varied talents necessary to be effective often are outside the scope of the venture capitalists. When the competition really gets tough, from foreign as well as domestic competitors, it takes deep pockets and patience to wait for the rewards of innovation. In this vein, Schlumberger was the perfect parent for a promising but troubled Fairchild Semiconductor acquired in 1979. Schlumberger could afford to ride out the interim ups and downs of the semiconductor business. For this giant company, it was an affordable opportunity, and in the long run one which may give it an enviable star to go with its primary business of well-drilling services.

There are a great number of other cases one could point to where crossing business lines make sense, at least as a formulation of strategy. Implementation is the point at which many concepts fail. The danger in relying on financial synergy alone is that while companies may complement each other's financial characteristics, an acquired firm may prove to be an operating disappointment. This was the case for many financially justified acquisitions in the late 1960s. With the disappearance of a favorable economic and financial environment in the 1970s, operating weaknesses were exposed and a period of divestments and strategic reappraisals ensued.

Financial synergy does not allow for strategic miscalculations in the performance of the acquired business. Because the parent company is not actively managing its acquisitions, the price paid must be justified from financial synergy alone: i.e., reduction of corporate risk, entry into better performing businesses, use of tax losses, or other financially-oriented advantages. The financial premiums realized must outweigh the premiums above market price — often running to 40 or 50 percent — that acquirors are forced to pay. The competition to acquire stars, cows, or speculative ventures in a diversified portfolio has eliminated the easy pickings.

Thus while a viable case for financial synergy can be made, by itself it lacks scope to explain the acquisition scene. It implies no change in operating efficiencies or direct control of the acquired company, and it further assumes the business is available at a "reasonable" purchase price. It does not deal with acquisitions lacking the conventional financial "fit." Indeed, many companies in mature industries have acquired companies in equally mature industries without the ability to recover the substantial premium paid over market if they pursued only a passive investment strategy. In order to derive the benefits from such actions, the acquiror has to "create" value in the acquired firm. This involves more than financial synergy. It requires management. Two additional approaches for creating synergy from an acquired business are discussed below.

SYNERGY FROM SKILLS TRANSFERENCE

One alternative for creating value is to exploit an undermanaged aspect of the acquired business. In such cases, acquirors can seek a performance premium by transferring a particular parent company skill, such as marketing, technology, distribution channels, or superior management. This transference of parent company competence can be used to reposition the acquired firm into a better competitive standing with enhanced market share. The process is often energized by financial resources the parent firm can provide.

The Marketing Push

A classic example of this type of synergy is Philip Morris's acquisition of Miller Beer. Only in seventh place in the brewing industry when acquired, Miller Beer now is solidly entrenched in second place. Using a combination of market segmentation skills common to Philip Morris's cigarette business, and a strong advertising and promotional campaign (most of us are familiar with Miller's sports-star television advertisements) Philip Morris vaunted this acquisition over its competitors. Previously competing on price and economies of scale from large efficient breweries, the brewing industry is now imitating Miller's basic strategy of market segmentation coupled with advertising and promotional support.

To sustain its advantage, however, Philip Morris also had to invest heavily in new capacity as its market share expanded. Thus the Miller acquisition required a transference of marketing skills, plus commitment of substantial financial resources to build and protect a higher market share. None of these attributes were characteristics of Miller Beer prior to its acquisition. Even if Miller Beer had been capable of raising the necessary capital, it lacked the marketing skills for this level of breakthrough. Without its acquisition by Philip Morris, Miller Beer's market share and performance would likely have continued their decline and its competitor ranking would have deteriorated even further.

A similar tactic may be envisioned by Procter & Gamble in acquiring Ben Hill Griffen, a citrus processor. Orange juice ranks behind only soft drinks and coffee in beverage sales. As was the case in Miller Beer, marketing is not the trademark of competition. The industry is typified by many unadvertised private-label brands and a history of low advertising by the branded market leaders, like Minute Maid, a product of Coca-Cola, and Beatrice Foods's Tropicana. Procter & Gamble's Citrus Hill brand hit the stores after just one year of testing, with a reported $75 to $100 million advertising budget in its first year. This is a quantum jump in advertising support, the most spent by far for a new brand of juice. Just as Miller Beer upset the balance in the beer industry by forcing brewers to focus on market segmentation and dramatically alter their basic strategy, Procter & Gamble undoubtedly will force some reaction from other juice processors.

One case where purchase of a lackluster performer obtained spectacular results was Chesebrough-Pond's 1969 acquisition of Ragu. Just $44 million in stock bought this small regional producer of spaghetti sauce. The acquisition raised obvious questions at the time. Why move an old-line company specializing in personal care products into the highly competitive food business? And why pick such an unlikely target with such seemingly limited potential?

As was the case with Philip Morris, Chesebrough-Pond's strategy encompassed a combination of transferred marketing skills to capitalize on the acquired company's undermanaged product potential, plus an infusion of capital to sustain a successful build-and-expand program. In this instance, as in Miller Beer, it was not the product itself that served as the basis for significant advantage, but rather the way the product was marketed. Chesebrough sought to capitalize on the fact that no brand of spaghetti sauce was marketed nationwide. Ragu spaghetti sauce revenues were $25 million when it was purchased. In just a few years, Ragu became the leading spaghetti sauce, accounting for nearly two of every three purchases, parlaying Chesebrough-Pond's modest stake into a dominant position in a field that exceeds $600 million in size and is projected to more than double by the end of this decade.

The basic idea used here was to launch a concerted advertising and promotional campaign to make Ragu a national brand. The components of the strategy were elementary: find a company with a good product in a limited regional market, introduce a mix of sophisticated marketing and money, and take it national. Chesebrough-Pond's pursued this fundamental approach with two subsequent acquisitions; Health-Tex, a regional manufacturer of children's clothing, and G. H. Bass, a regional producer of shoes famed for its "penny loafers." In both cases, the price was right, the strategy based on skill transference and expansion, and the resulting growth and return on investment exceptional.

Redefining the Base

An enticing target for the skill-transference idea of a Chesebrough-Pond's are industries where *no national brands exist*. In these situations, the skills of an acquiring company are introduced into the industry by way of acquisition and used to gain high performance results by taking the acquired company "national." A contrasting, but also successful, strategy is possible by intensive application of skills within a defined geographic market. G. Heileman Brewing Company, for example, built a successful wholesale bakery business through acquisitions confined to its home market in the Midwest. Despite the maturity of the bakery business, Heileman achieved very satisfactory performance by first buying assets cheaply, generally below replacement cost, and then transferring skills in distribution and management to utilize these assets more efficiently than the former owners did. Although two separate industries, the brewing and bakery business share similar distribution methods, with both products enjoying frequent purchase, and both having the potential for creating distribution scale economies as well as barriers to entry. Extending this apparent logic, Heileman also acquired Barrel O'Fun, a snack food manufacturer and distributor.

In all of the above illustrations, financial resources were integral to achieving a synergistic effect: to support a new marketing, distribution, or product strategy, and ultimately to invest in new capacity to gain market share. Thus financial synergy still makes up part of the "skill" strategy, but it alone is an insufficient formula for success. If it were, the companies that were acquired could have borrowed the funds and enjoyed the rewards themselves. Certainly for the leading and profitable firms in the beer industry at the time of the Miller Beer acquisition (Anheuser-Busch, Schlitz, and Coors), finances were not restricting strategy. Moreover, if financial synergy alone could produce such results, then the performance of holding companies would be much better than their record shows.

Clearly, the critical element in these cases is the transference of a specific skill from the parent to the acquired company. A further aspect of such an approach is to acquire a business for a price that *does not already discount its potential*. Once acquired, the performance is then raised — not through direct product or market combinations, but by the transference of parent company skills and a perspective for strategic advantage.

RESTRUCTURING INTO STRATEGIC GROUPS

Conglomerates that have been engaged in an active diversification program can find synergy through restructuring these various businesses into strategic groupings. These groups become the focus of the firm's strategic plan and form the "cores" around which smaller, related acquisitions can be added to form a desired critical mass. In the process, old industry boundaries erode, new industry groupings are formed, and new potentials for operating efficiencies are created. This is, however, a largely uncharted process. There is, to my knowledge, no company that has been successful in achieving a perfect *rationalization*, or balance, of its strategic groups of businesses. There are, on the other hand, a great number of conglomerates currently restructuring in search of a better balance among existing groupings.

Beatrice Foods, for example, accumulated six candy companies as part of its massive attempt at diversifying away from its original dairy business. Each candy business was managed independently, but none was sufficiently large to compete with industry majors like Mars Company. Beatrice planned to reorganize the six independent candy manufacturers into a single company with a single profit center. This would centralize marketing, sales, and distribution functions. The reorganization would lead to greater operating efficiencies and literally create a large new competitor in the candy industry. This concept was never brought to fruition, though, as Beatrice Foods instead put its acquisition program into an even higher gear by acquiring the diversified consumer-goods company, Esmark, and mapping a new round of realignments and divestments — including the sale of its candy business to the Hutomaki Group of Helsinki, Finland.

Allied Corporation, another conglomerate, is building a strategic group in the medical supply field through a combination of acquiring companies plus providing research and development resources from the parent. In 1981, Allied purchased Fisher Scientific, a supplier of laboratory equipment, instruments, and chemicals. Instrumentation Laboratory, a maker of medical and industrial instruments, was acquired in 1983. These two acquisitions form the nucleus of the Health and Scientific Products group. Allied will also devote the parent company's R&D resources to improve the competitive potential of this operation. And with Allied's reputation, further acquisitions should not be ruled out.

Finally, R.J. Reynolds Industries provides an example of a company that has the makings of new diversified food and beverage groups in its mix of acquired businesses. As described earlier, Reynolds's purchase of Del Monte in 1979 provided a major upward move for its formerly modest stake in food and beverages. Reynolds's subsequent acquisition of Heublein further strengthened its position. This combined food-and-beverage sector was placed under a single top executive. Thus a logical next step would be to organize this bunch of loosely related businesses into one or more strategic groups. R. J. Reynolds's has already completed an upgrading and integration of Del Monte with its own food and beverage units, including large investments to modernize facilities and raise productivity. It now faces the more difficult and time-consuming task of integrating the parts of each acquisition into a cohesive organization, with compatible pairings of businesses, creating strong operating units.

Lacking the guidance of a strategical map to follow, companies have relied heavily on instincts and judgment to form new and effective structures. Companies like Litton, AMF, Beatrice Foods, and RCA have restructured not once, but several times. Each period involved a new rationalization and a new learning experience. But this is a long and painful way to gain knowledge. Obviously, it would be preferable to tailor actions to suit designs. As a first step, companies must weigh the expected synergies from acquisitions against the type of distinctive competence brought by the acquirer. This observation, so fundamental to a successful strategy, has often been lacking in practice.

The Issue of Competence

In entering a new business, companies must seek a comparative advantage. Conglomerates should form strategic groups in businesses where they have a distinctive competence and exit from those areas in which competitors have the edge. In the process, a considerable reshuffling of assets will ensue over a considerable length of time until the desired groupings are achieved. Profitability itself will provide the pressure for corporations to specialize, a principle as old as Adam Smith. In this case, however, it is not specialization of product but specialization of managerial resources within a particular market. With varying types of specialization, companies will strive for different characteristics in their strategic groups. And what is a desirable competitive arena for one company may be undesirable for another.

General Electric, for instance, agreed in 1983 to sell its small housewares operations to Black and Decker. For General Electric, this move furthered its strategic plan to emphasize high-growth and high-technology areas. For Black and Decker, the advantages were a major step up in size, a strong position in small household appliances, and the diversification it has been seeking to broaden its product base away from dependence on power tools. In a similar incident, Continental Group sold more than $500 million in containerboard and kraft paper assets to Stone Container. This catapults Stone into the top five companies producing corrugated containers and multi-wall bags. Perhaps as important, the cost to build equivalent capacity would have been more than several times Stone's purchase price. Continental Group, already a conglomerate, received money to reinvest into businesses it believes offer more promise than those it sold. *

When Dow Chemical brought Richardson-Merrell's ethical drug line it looked on it as an option to the commodity side of its chemical business. Richardson-Merrell saw it as an opportunity to escape a field that had given it repeated headaches, low profits, and required more R&D dollars than the company could justify. Moreover, Richardson-Merrell performed much better in the over-the-counter market with such famous brand names as Vicks and Oil of Olay. Subsequently, Dow is trying to expand its prescription drug business and Richardson-Vicks (its new name) has seen earnings take a turn for the better. This type of cross-switching into and out of businesses can be beneficial to both parties. It is a matter of upgrading in areas of company strength and eliminating businesses with less potential. The following figure illustrates the match between a company's distinctive competences and desired synergies.

In sum, synergy comes in a variety of forms, just as diversification itself. Financial synergy is the easiest to achieve, but is also the one with the lowest long-term payout. Skill transference is a second order of synergy and can be achieved by selective implanting of a parent company's special competence into an acquired firm. This stops short of a major overhaul of the acquired operations, but can provide the stimulus for a rebirth of growth and expansion. Finally, major restructuring into new industry groups offers

---

*Continental Group subsequently was itself acquired by a private investor.

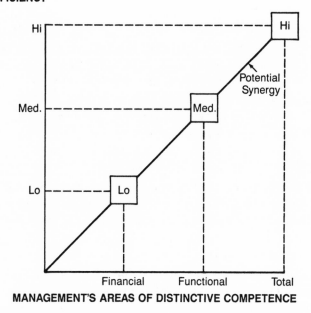

Distinctive Competence, Organizational Efficiency and Potential Synergy

long-term synergy of another sort. It requires melding many smaller, unrelated businesses into a coherent "family" of related business groups. It also places the greatest demands on management in terms of integrating companies with different cultures, making difficult cost reduction decisions, and developing controls to handle the widespread diversity of operations. But the compensations can be correspondingly high.

THE INTEGRATED CONGLOMERATE: THE ULTIMATE STRATEGY

A final, critical aspect of a successful diversification is time for the acquired business to become part of a unified organization. This element of success eludes first-time diversifiers. At the beginning, organizational efficiency is traded for better allocation of cash flows as a company acquires unfamiliar businesses and introduces foreign cultures. Sometimes the shock of transforming is too great and the company reverts to its former stance.

Such "culture shock" has been especially prevalent in high-tech acquisitions. Lured by the promise of fast growth and exotic new technologies, large companies have snapped up smaller technologically oriented firms. In many such cases, the entrepreneurial spirit that fueled these small, feisty companies was smothered by the bureaucratic routine of the acquiror. As a sample, Raytheon acquired Lexitron, a leader in word processing, in 1978. By 1983, after pouring tens of millions of dollars into the venture, Raytheon took a large write-off and sold the unit, with other parts of its Data Systems Division, to Telex. Raytheon claimed it couldn't recruit engineers to work for Lexitron because it was associated with the parent, whose major business was seen as "defense." Outsiders, including personnel from Lexitron itself, felt that Raytheon made a number of managerial mistakes and never really understood the business. In the end, the specific reasons didn't much matter. The overriding point was Raytheon's attraction to product synergies alone, without regard for the organizational problems of managing a completely different and innovative business. Even where successful, the integration of a new business may take decades. Without preparation for this side of diversification, synergy will remain an unfulfilled potential.

The figure on page 61 is a more formal representation of an instinctively reasonable association between competence, synergy, and organizational efficiency. The gist is that a company's diversification efforts should be guided by its distinctive competence and its expectations tempered by the time and management effort required for a specific level of synergy. Interestingly, the greatest potential is the most difficult and uncertain path to pursue. This reflects the entertwining of risk with reward.

In the following figure, the components of the figure on page 61 are reconstructed in order to emphasize the time dimension. In period one, for instance, a company is just starting the long journey of evolving into a mature conglomerate, and its initial moves create stress on the existing organizational structure. During periods of active diversification, organizational efficiency is at a minimum. This drop in overall performance must be compensated for by better internal options for allocation of financial resources.

Thus unrelated diversification involves both good news and bad news. Until a company learns to manage and integrate its acquisitions, it is dependent on autonomous units operating profitably enough to overcome the lack of administrative coordination. This leaves the company vulnerable to unexpected downturns in the new businesses which it cannot directly

Tradeoffs in Implementing a Strategy of Unrelated Diversification

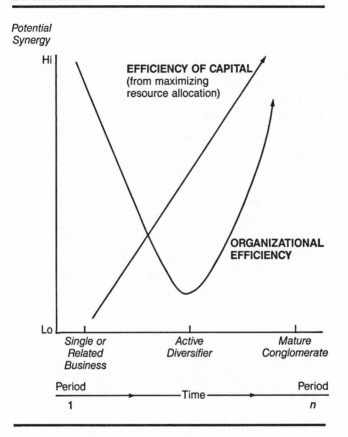

control nor totally avoid. Over time, the level of administrative control tends to rise. If this aspect of diversification is mastered, and an optimum "family" of businesses emerges, then the fruits of the labor of diversification can be enjoyed. Getting there is obviously the tricky part. The task for top managers is to anticipate the trials of organizational restructuring as well as the higher returns from repositioning into more attractive markets.

Total integration — the optimum synergy — is not a realistic goal for all companies. It requires the broadest managerial scope and control of new businesses. It suggests competence in strategic planning, organizational restructuring, and general management. It further requires a significant period of time to integrate the acquiror and the acquiree. Clearly, all companies are not equally capable of handling this variety of demands. If a firm is endowed with financial resources, but its managers are experienced only in a narrow line of business, diversification will be a risky undertaking and should not be considered unless the alternatives are stark.

When U.S. Leasing diversified in 1978, for example, it gave a plausible reason. Its core business — buying and leasing office equipment — appeared to have limited potential. As a first step in a new direction, the firm bought a savings and loan company, presumably a solid base on which to layer other investments. But this "anchor" almost pulled U.S. Leasing under as the thrift industry entered a stressful and profitless period. Jettisoning this acquisition four years later, the company saw its prosaic old business in a new light. It abandoned its pretense of becoming a conglomerate and concentrated its energies on raising the return in its leasing business and ended by building a stronger, more competitive leasing company.

This story underlines the importance of having a plan before attempting a strategy. Without a distinctive competence in running a savings and loan firm, nor the financial resources to ride out a storm, nor a strategic vision of what to do next, U.S. Leasing was much better off staying where it was. Diversification is not a solution for every company with a problem. If a company's competence and management style are uniquely tied to its present line of business, then it is probably best to remain where it is. If all companies were competent to manage every industry, there would be no one to buy. The principle of comparative advantage rests on distinctive competences being unevenly distributed and an abundance of inefficiencies to attack. Skills are brought to bear on problems, and the process results in more efficient allocation of resources.

Industry Structures and Life Cycles:
The Search for New Markets

Because the most dramatic payoff in synergy assumes the forming of new strategic groups, the question of what determines 'appropriateness' in a strategic group naturally arises. Oddly enough, conjecture on what constitutes an 'appropriate' competitive arena for companies has drawn little interest from either theorists or practitioners. A traditional approach still emphasizes competition within existing industry structures. This viewpoint, however, does not deal directly with the question posed by conglomerates: What are the right industries to be in? The justification for organizing has always been economic; that is, whether a firm offers cheaper, better, or more desirable products or services. In this context, genealogy is not an issue. Only the circumstance of a company's beginnings, and the imprint of this fact on theory, suggest that a firm's future should be tied to its past. If Andrew Carnegie were reincarnated, it is unlikely that he would start out to recreate U.S. Steel. Given the new tools of strategic management, it is more likely that managers who think big would think of diversifying to maximize performance and minimize risks.

Are some companies uniquely qualified to manage in more than one major business? Is competition and consumer welfare promoted or harmed by the stability of industry structures? These questions have never been seriously studied, but an implicit response has been given by the many companies making acquisitions outside their core businesses. Companies seek to grow. By staying within a single industry, the prospects for growth eventually diminish. When asked, top managers repeatedly cite return on capital as their primary objective, without mention of industry structures. As long as industry structures offer profitable investment for capital, there is no urgency to look outside them.

Over time, however, high growths and profitability become more elusive. It is when industries begin to show the effects of age that diversification

Life Cycle Possibilities and Patterns

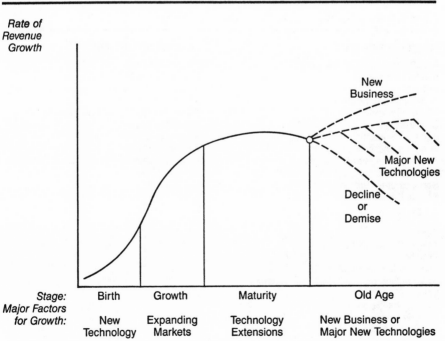

pressures build. Each product, company, and industry has a life cycle. From the first sale, a new product or service has a measured life that follows a cycle of innovation, growth, maturity, and decline, as in the following figure. The length of each period varies, but the pattern is immutable. New markets are the force driving companies to expand initially, with new technology sustaining the growth momentum. As organizations grow, so does the weight and inertia of current operations. Peter Drucker has postulated that every product is "right" for thirty or forty years. Given this time horizon, many of today's large corporations formed more than three-quarters of a century ago undoubtedly face the less attractive slope of the life cycle in "old" product lines (see the following table).

Diversification is no substitute, however, for managing current assets for their utmost potential. Japanese firms have repeatedly forced U.S. companies to reexamine assumptions of so-called market maturity. Radios are an example where U.S. manufacturers almost abandoned new investments in this line, until the Japanese discovered a new path to profits. The Japanese didn't treat radios as a type of hardware. By ignoring blind acceptance of a static life cycle, they pioneered a new category of products.

Life Cycle Stages of Various Industry Groups

"OLDER INDUSTRIES"

Agriculture and fisheries
Alcoholic beverages
Apparel
Printing and publishing
Wholesale trade
Construction
Bottled and canned soft drinks
Furniture and fixtures
Nonmetallic mineral products
Other and miscellaneous manufacturing
Services other than motion pictures
Ship and boat building

"EMERGING INDUSTRIES"

Biotechnology
Telecommunications
Robotics
Semiconductors/Electronics
Satellite Communications/Data Transmission
Fiber Optics
Artificial Intelligence
Genetic Engineering
Microprocessors

"NEWER INDUSTRIES"

Pharmaceuticals
Household applicances
Radio and television broadcasting
Motor transportation
Office, computing, and accounting machines
Aircraft and parts
Air transportation
Scientific, measuring, and control devices

Untroubled by the idea that the radios as hardware had peaked out, they studied the times, places, and occasions of such consumer behavior as listening to broadcasts, recording, and listening to recorded music, and they drew an entirely different conclusion. The resulting floods of composite products, such as radio cassettes and Sony's Walkman, are history. The fact that American consumers are actually buying these products in such numbers is decisive proof that user needs, latent or explicit, were there all the time.[1]

In a somewhat similar case of revision, Foremost McKesson, the nation's largest wholesale distributor, had come close to selling off its drug wholesaling business — its largest segment — because manufacturers increasingly were distributing their own wares. It seemed like a classic case of obsolescence. Foremost McKesson's own customers were siphoning off its profits. But things brightened when Foremost McKesson decided to take a strategically different view of the problem. What if it added new technology to its traditional services, and thus became more cost-effective than its customers? Foremost McKesson rethought and redefined its basic strategy. With the aid of new computer assisted services, it transformed itself into a "superwholesaler." In the process, it preserved its role as a middleman.

The search for new strategies in old markets is obviously important. New technologies can rejuvenate "mature" businesses and the R&D effort should be unrelenting. But innovation can be carried on in a number of different businesses as well as in a single business. Diversification can be used to advantage, for example, by centralizing parts of the R&D process, to achieve economies of scale, while diversifying widely the number of possible product markets for investment. On the other hand, commitment to a mature business with hopes of inventing a new technology, or discovering a new market, can be a more problematic course of action. For some companies, diversification is a means of survival.

In extreme cases, unrelated diversification may be the only escape from disaster. Insilco, for example, exchanged a tenuous position in silverware for a new future in high tech. Formerly the International Silver Company, its origins date back to the early 1800s, when it made silver and pewter spoons and dishes. Since the 1970s, however, low priced imports, inflated silver prices, and changing American lifestyles doomed Insilco's dream of maintaining a high growth image. It could have limped along, surviving on the margin of prosperity. It even might have hoped for a reversal, if favorable trends in silver prices or lifestyles returned. But why risk it? All the literature on strategic management suggests that managers *plan* their future rather than wait for it to be thrust on them. The dark clouds in Insilco's future were in view. It was only a matter of time before the company got rained on. Insilco's maneuvering for a new vision of the company has included some questionable acquisitions and a checkered record of performance. But in the end its choices may enable it to survive better than clinging to a fading domestic market.

Singer is another company that barely woke up in time to the perils of a shrinking core business. It, too, lived through treacherous experiences with unsuccessful acquisitions. Whether its current focus on aerospace proves profitable is a matter of speculation. It is an option, however, that every manager, employee, and shareholder of Singer should prefer to the prospect of being back in the shrunken market for sewing machines.

The ability to shape the future is what distinguishes the so-called new strategic management from the old "crisis" management. Managers are supposed to ask themselves what business they should be in — not plan around whatever business they find themselves stuck with. This means planning exits as well as exploiting new markets. The time for exiting a business is before it becomes an obvious necessity. U.S. Steel's shares once sold for over $100 per share. It could have acquired almost any company it wanted at that time, and almost anything it bought would have proved a better investment than steel. Diversification would have been a low-risk alternative in this case. Even without the aid of hindsight, the storm clouds ahead for steel were clear to many objective observers. Waiting too long to begin a diversification program is perhaps the greatest single mistake for companies faced with a hostile environment.

A NEW WAY TO COMPETE

Just as the elimination of hypothetical industry barriers changes the way companies organize, a crossing of national boundaries into world markets changes the way companies compete. Steel and other "old" U.S. industries have today become the "new" industries of foreign countries with lower costs of labor and materials. In a global sense, U.S. Steel and other domestic steel producers have lost their comparative advantage. From a strictly economic view, domestic steel production can be justified only in the specialized or high technology ends of the business. The commodity products of steel — the plain bars, rods, and sheets — can be produced more cheaply abroad. The long term outlooks are not good. Companies with large commodity-type businesses must strive to reposition themselves away from generic products with low skill requirements.

For companies in the relatively "new" industries, the need to diversify is less urgent. Firms like IBM and Merck have tremendous growth and opportunity in their own businesses. It is difficult to conceive of unrelated markets that could achieve the performance these firms already enjoy. In the case of Merck, the largest drug company in the U.S., early diversification forays into water treatment and kelp harvesting proved unproductive, and references to such acquisitions are no longer a prominent part of its annual report to shareholders. Such premature attempts at unrelated diversification underscore the importance of timing. Diversifying too early invites the risk of mismanaging new businesses and diverting resources from more attractive core businesses. This type of strategic error can be just as damaging as diversifying too late.

For managers, the future is never totally clear, but the lessons of the past provide some valuable clues. First, the range of strategic options narrows as a company grows. Timing of diversification is critical. With perfect foresight, diversification would begin at the apex of a market cycle, as illustrated in the figure on page 65. Realistically, companies would do well to recognize the *need* for diversification, stressing internal mechanisms to increase efficiency more than the precise timing of the moves.

A second unequivocal message of history is that evolution is a dynamic process and that static methods of analysis, no matter how inventive, will eventually warp the strategy of those who rely unblinkingly on them. No single prescriptive model can capture all the multidimensions and time phases appropriate for every company's situation. Orienting managers' thinking toward a range of alternatives and environments is accomplishment enough. Once alerted, managers themselves are responsible for devising specific solutions to fit their organization.

Notes

1. Kenichi Ohmae, *The Mind of the Strategist.* New York: McGraw-Hill, 1982, p. 152.

Part Two

THE MANAGEMENT CHALLENGE

4 ORGANIZING FOR DIVERSITY

M ANAGING A CONGLOMERATE is like teaching an elephant to dance. It's not easy and it takes a long time to learn. So far, progress on this all-important aspect of successful diversification has been slow. While certain strategic keys have been accepted, how to implement them organizationally remains elusive.

Most conglomerates are in a transitional phase, between the initiation of a major new strategy and development of the organizational structure to reflect it. Some are just beginning their program of diversification. Others have yet to achieve the desired spread into new businesses. Strategy is still being refined in these cases, and thus postpones establishment of permanent structural changes.

The time it takes to master new structures is also affected by the uniqueness of the conglomerate strategy. The longer a company stays with an existing strategy and structure, the more resistant it becomes to doing things differently. When the first conglomerate pioneers emerged in the 1950s, their apparent acts of random diversification did not invite imitation among the conservative leadership of big business. Only relatively recently has the strategy of conglomerates gained this endorsement. Consequently, attention to the management of multi-industry firms has still a way to evolve.

The overall pattern, however, resembles the lessons of history. Entrepreneurial managers experiment with new strategies, and are followed by administrators who perfect the internal mechanisms of control. Those companies that don't adjust administratively risk failure. During the intense consolidation-type mergers around the turn of the century, for example, a loose holding company arrangement maintained minimum operating controls over the many constituent firms until management could bond the various units into a single, cohesive structure. In the end, however, according to Alfred Chandler, "mergers quickly found themselves in financial difficulty if they remained merely holding companies." Few mergers achieved long-term profitability unless a managerial hierarchy capable of managing the merger strategy evolved. Conglomerate mergers should prove no exception. Without structural match-ups with strategy, the synergy from diversification will fall short of the full potential illustrated by the figure on page 63 in chapter three.

Even now, after considerable time devoted to improving the strategy of unrelated diversification, the structural component of management's task is an Achilles heel for conglomerates. There have been isolated experiments, and accomodations on a case-by-case basis, but there are no established principles of organization designed for conglomerates or companies aspiring to become conglomerates.

OLD METHODS:
THE MULTI-DIVISIONAL STRUCTURE

There have been two major structural innovations in big business: organization by function and by division (as illustrated in the chart opposite). The first was developed to handle the strategy of giant size. Firms were organized around managers who specialized in such functions as marketing, production, accounting, finance, etc. This achieved economies of specialization and worked well as long as companies remained with a single business.

The divisional structure reflected the switch to a strategy of related diversification. As companies moved away from a core business, the argument for restructuring around distinct business units became more powerful. By dividing a firm into divisions, for instance, profit responsibility could be centered in divisional managers. This delegated more autonomy to the business level while retaining control of operations at headquarters. Companies could keep growing by hiring new divisional heads to manage the spread into related businesses. By the 1920s, a multi-divisional structure had become the most widely employed in big business, and it remains the dominant design for managing diversified companies today.

The difficulty arises when trying to accomodate the new, rather unorthodox strategy of conglomerates with a structure designed long ago and

Two Basic Organizational Structures

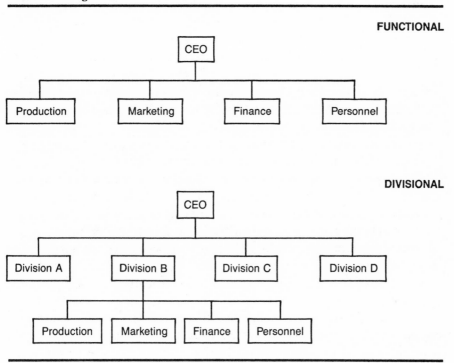

for a different purpose. Because the multi-divisional structure owes much to a military style of organizing, a military analogy can be useful in explaining the shortcomings of such a structure for conglomerates.

A multi-divisional structure is like a pyramid with the generals at the top, the line commanders in the middle, and the lesser officers and troops reporting to them. Karl Von Clausewitz, the Prussian strategist, is the architect of this type of organization. Von Clausewitz's concept of strategy was imbued with his knowledge of war and tactics, staffs and lines of command. His was an instinctively appealing organization for business to copy. Divisions, regiments, battalions, companies, platoons, and squads all pull together in order to win wars. Sectors, groups, divisions, departments, and plants should do likewise to win the competitive battles waged in the marketplace.

However, when companies step outside their competitive arenas and take on new foes on foreign terrain with a different cast of supporting units, the best appproach to strategy may not be the old one. To continue the military analogy, managing a conglomerate is more like managing an army of allies rather than a single unified force. As commander-in-chief of the Allied forces responsible for the invasion of Europe towards the end of World War II, General Dwight Eisenhower fought on two fronts. In addition to planning for the invasion, he had to pick the officers to head the various Allied units and meld them into an effective organization while dealing with autonomy-seeking commanders like Field Marshall Montgomery of Britain and General Charles DeGaulle of France. Eisenhower was at one point prepared to resign in frustration. Managing the war had become harder than actually fighting it.

Corporations have copied the military model in terms of building tight, *integrated* organizations. Strong controls emanate from the top. As companies diversify, some decentralization of authority occurs. But major operating and diversification decisions still flow to the top. This type of diversification can be handled without completely overhauling the administrative system. For example, DuPont, a model of a decentralized multidivisional corporation, was in 1921 participating in five separate lines of business, but all could be traced to a "root" chemical technology and none was dramatically afield from DuPont's areas of managerial and operating expertise.

Dividing the firm into operating divisions was a means of handling *related* diversification. As companies expanded their product lines, they were reorganized to reflect the distinctions among different products and markets. Divisions became more autonomous, but companies continued to have a strong operational bias. Structure followed strategy, as Chandler posits, but the strategy remained oriented to building an integrated organization that was diversifying gradually from within or from acquisitions related to a core business. Diversification was concentric rather than conglomerate. Wholesale and rapid restructuring into completely new businesses was not part of that pattern.

MODERN CONGLOMERATES NEED
MODERN STRUCTURES

The radical nature of the new conglomerate strategy contrasted with the tradition of strategy being "just a little ahead" of structure. The previous strategies of size and related diversification built on one another in modular fashion. Conglomerates, on the other hand, were in total and fundamental contrast with what had gone before, growing into completely different industries seemingly overnight. This sharp distinction in strategy called for much more than marginal adjustments in structure.

Another disruptive aspect of the conglomerate strategy was the cyclical nature of restructuring. Companies don't become conglomerates in a single bold stroke. Diversification tends to come in waves, sometimes with long intervals between major growth cycles. Such "broken" patterns of diversification are sometimes hidden in trend lines that show a continuous increase in activity. For instance, the collective move of companies into unrelated businesses has been a persistent trend since the mid-1950s. Yet within this broad movement, there have been several distinct "waves" of conglomerate activity led by a new cast of firms each time. Actively diversifying companies consist of several different groups of firms at different times and not, as might appear from casual observation, a united front of companies moving in coordination.

In effect, older conglomerates mature and moderate their diversification activity, while newer conglomerates-to-be are embarking on their programs of diversification. During this process, companies experiment in order to find the right strategic position. This often involves divestment of past acquisitions and a refocusing of strategy on fewer and larger strategic groups of businesses. Such shifts in strategy upset the timetable for organizational stability as well. Only after fluctuations in strategy subside can stable and permanent structures be contemplated.

A final dilemma presented by the conglomerate phenomenon is how to establish competitive strategies for existing businesses while keeping an eye on strategy aimed at changing the mix of businesses. This represents the challenge of managing for stability and change at the same time. Dual levels of management and planning are involved. Few, if any, diversified companies have come up with a satisfactory means for combining the necessary mix of flexibility and integration in a conglomerate structure. Having invented conglomerates, managers still seem undecided on how best to organize to deal with their complexities.

What organizational implications do the above shifts in strategy imply? How is the conglomerate concept going to affect organizational design of companies who are striving to become diversified? The final details will be clear only after a sufficient number of firms have made their choice of strategies. There will be a range of different approaches reflecting the number and types of companies that are restructuring. In general, however, two points seem clear:

1. A long adjustment period will be necessary.

2. The advantages of tightly integrated operations must be *temporarily* abandoned.

The experimental nature of conglomerate strategy has deterred more progress from being made toward stable organizational solutions. But since conglomerates aren't going to go away, the pressure for administrative reforms will continue to build. The question is not whether structures will adapt, but when and how. What seems a safe assumption is that a long learning period and perhaps more than one round of changes will be necessary to make the transition to a desired level of diversity. Companies take different paths at different times in diversifying. What works for one is not necessarily appropriate for another. Also, since reaching the desired state of diversity involves a number of cycles, the entire process may extend over many years for an individual firm, or over many decades for big business as a whole.

Secondly, the move to where a company wants to be from where it began requires abandoning old ways and learning new techniques. The benefits of an integrated organization, for example, must be traded off temporarily for the quite separate advantages of unrelated diversification. This means more reliance on the synergies associated with diversification and less emphasis on internal growth alone. Furthermore, it means shifting to different structures as strategy dictates.

For instance, the holding company structure has been associated with conglomerates because many conglomerates adopted this structure first. As companies moved aggressively into a number of different businesses, each was operated as an autonomous unit bonded together with the parent company mainly by financial ties. This style of organization was typical of failed attempts to build large consolidated empires — especially in the utility industry — in the 1920s and 1930s. As Chandler had observed, companies that didn't progress toward building operating synergies in mergers were unsuccessful in the long-term. Likewise, conglomerates that stay with a holding company structure in which major businesses are operated autonomously will have difficulty. Many early conglomerates, like ITT and City Investing, had great problems making the transition from a loose federation of unrelated businesses to an integrated company made up of strategic business groups. Today, conglomerates that cannot or will not impose managerial discipline on their various businesses, as in the case of holding companies that preceded them, will underperform as a whole.

Most diversified companies, however, have long since advanced beyond this initial structure. To continue to associate conglomerates with the holding company structure of the past is to ignore the necessity for the dynamics of structure to reflect the dynamics of strategy. There are wide disparities between the mature conglomerate and the diversifying novice. Difficult interim choices must be made between an integrated structure suited for a mature conglomerate and a loose holding company arrangement of a neophyte. Here are four illustrative prototypes of organizational structure representative of different points along such an evolutionary journey (see the following figure).

Type I: Active Diversifiers

Beatrice is at one end of the diversification spectrum. Beatrice has been trying to decide what it wants to be by buying and shedding companies since the 1950s. Beginning as a dairy in Beatrice, Nebraska in 1894, the company exploded into a multibillion-dollar conglomerate ninety years later. Along the way, it has made most of the early conglomerates look like pikers.

Beatrice acquired hundreds of companies in the 1950s and 1960s but did not divest itself of businesses it acquired, nor did it attempt to impose centralized controls. By 1979, Beatrice had 430 profit centers and no effective means of managing them as a single corporation. With a new chief executive officer in that same year, Beatrice's strategy began to change. It initiated a program of divesting as well as one of acquiring. It targeted 56 businesses for sale with more than $1 billion in revenues, including Dannon Yogurt, one of its best known brands. It also made two significant acquisitions: Coca-Cola Bottling of Los Angeles, and Buckingham, a liquor importer.

In 1982, Beatrice took another strategic tack. Desiring to transform its image from a sprawling conglomerate into a giant diversified company known for its marketing expertise, Beatrice planned to consolidate into six major groups and slim down to between fifty to seventy businesses.

Then in 1984 along came Esmark. Itself a conglomerate, Esmark had acquired Norton Simon, a company diversified into cosmetics, food, and auto leasing. Beatrice, a $9.3 – billion conglomerate, announced its desire to acquire Esmark, a $4.1 – billion conglomerate, with the expectation of creating a multifaceted, consumer-oriented, marketing-driven enterprise. The chief executive of Beatrice claimed, "It's the final seal on what we've been trying to do." Others were not so sure. It obviously meant a heroic

Four Organizational Designs for Diversified Firms (by stage of diversification)

TYPE I — Holding Company Design: No Integration of Businesses (i.e., Beatrice)

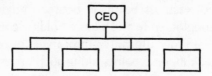

TYPE II — Transitional Company Design: Integrated Core Business with Independent Subsidiaries (i.e., Coca-Cola)

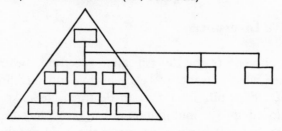

TYPE III — Transitional Company Design: Partially Integrated with no Single Dominant Business (i.e., United Technologies)

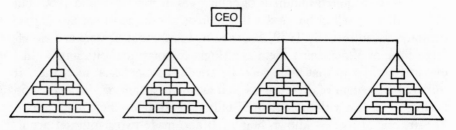

TYPE IV — Mature Conglomerate: Total Integration of Operations (i.e., General Electric)

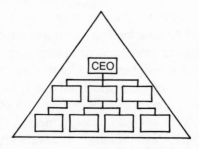

new round of divestments — while holding on to what still fit — to pay the high cost of the acquisition. As justification for its action, Beatrice pointed to Esmark's distribution, research, and sales organization as boosting Beatrice's own largely regional businesses. Duplicating those assets, Beatrice's CEO felt, would have taken "five years and untold millions to put into place."

Whatever the merits of Beatrice's strategy prove to be in the future, it clearly has a long way to go before integrating all the pieces it has acquired. Even assuming no major added acquisitions, the task of divesting and realigning its current businesses is immense. With the addition of new businesses come new managers from different cultures and with different values. Given these factors, along with Beatrice's own internal management problems due to its volatile nature, it is in for a long period of digestion. At present it could not, and should not, try to emulate a traditional integrated administrative structure. It must make progress slowly.

For a company like Beatrice, a formal administrative system is not its first concern. Its priorities clearly are to develop a strategic grouping of businesses first, and then decide how they can best be cohesively managed. While the first part of this process is being actively pursued, progress on the second will undoubtedly be slow. Synergy must come primarily from the financial impetus of being in the "right" businesses or getting out of the "wrong" ones, and in allocating resources more effectively among the greater number of business alternatives under management's control. A holding company structure is appropriate at this particular stage. While financial and planning controls are much more sophisticated now than they were in the 1920s and 1930s, holding companies still depend largely on the wisdom of the choice of businesses and managers, not direct involvement in operations from corporate headquarters. And as long as acquirors keep their new businesses at arm's length, relying on financial relationships for synergy, a passive holding company approach to management is indicated. This is a common first step for first diversifiers getting used to managing new businesses. In Beatrice's case, it is a necessity forced on it by the massive and almost instantaneous creation of a sprawling enterprise. In style, Beatrice's approach resembles the 1950s "instant" conglomerate.

Type IV: Mature Conglomerates

A mature conglomerate is one that has absorbed its new businesses. Its diversification into different businesses is largely complete, and future growth depends on the current mix. GE is the epitome of this type of firm. It scores very high on "complexity" because of its presence in many different areas, but the degree of "changeability" is low because its emphasis is on operating its current businesses.

A mature conglomerate like GE is tightly integrated, with strong direction and review of operations from the top combined with a traditional decentralized, multi-divisional structure. Diversification has been gradual and primarily from within. This allowed incremental adjustments. Consequently, GE's administrative structure is as carefully layered as a wedding cake. Departments report to divisions, divisions report to groups, groups report to sectors, and sectors report to the executive office. Each layer of management is tied to the next and, ultimately, to the chief executive office. Such integration assures that each operating unit feels a part of, and identifies with, the corporation. Within this integrated structure, on the other hand, GE tries to give its managers room to exercise initiative. To spur innovativeness, GE has encouraged its managers to take risks and liberalized leeway for mistakes. But there is no question as to where the ultimate authority lies, nor what the consequences of too many avoidable mistakes are.

Over time, GE has melded its many disparate businesses into a cohesive *operating* company. The greatest synergy comes from the general management of all of its parts. Internal efficiency is therefore crucial. Monitoring of businesses is also critical, whereas the financially oriented diversifier compensates for looser controls by improving the mix of acquisitions. In a Type IV mature conglomerate a pervasive "culture" envelops all of the business groups and encloses them within a conventional pyramidal structure.

GE's inside-out approach to diversification is unique. Reliance on internal diversification for major repositioning into unrelated businesses is extremely rare nowadays. The great majority of firms diversify through acquisitions. Harold Geneen's many years of experience at the helm of ITT with many different companies has led him to observe "that as a matter of business judgment and for virtually all situations of real diversification into unrelated businesses this [internal diversification] is impractical and uneconomic and just will not happen."[1] Even Procter & Gamble, an avowed believer in internal diversification, recanted and has acquired soft drink, drug, and fruit juice businesses.

Each major unrelated acquisition tends to dilute the effectiveness of an existing integrated structure. Completing the evolutionary cycle and becoming a mature conglomerate generally involves many such moves. Thus, although GE's organizational structure represents a goal other diversified companies may eventually reach, it is a premature "model" for an interim stage of evolution typical of most diversifiers.

Unfortunately, GE is a ubiquitous example used to demonstrate su-
periority in all aspects of strategic management, including organization. Its
innovations have mistakenly been imitated by other conglomerates hoping
to copy GE's apparent success. Thus, as GE moved from a "group" to
"sector" type of management in 1977, other diversified firms followed suit.
But GE's organization is not a design for all contingencies. A sector merely
adds another layer to a traditional multidivisional structure. It deepens, but
does not otherwise change, the basic design. GE needed to relieve top
managers from the crush of responsibilities that had mushroomed as GE
grew. Managers previously reporting to the executive office now report to
sector executives. As a means for distributing an ever-growing workload,
it was a necessary and inventive idea. Asking it also to solve the problem
of rapid and transitional change would be expecting too much.

Types II and III: Transitional Diversifiers

The majority of conglomerates or aspiring conglomerates fall somewhere in
between the two extremes of a GE or a Beatrice. Some of the early ex-
perimenters, like Textron* and FMC, are closer to mature conglomerates,
in that diversification activity has slowed down and growth is expected to
come primarily from existing operations. But the slowing down has been
comparatively recent. These companies still face an adjustment period before transforming themselves into integrated operating companies.

New diversifiers like Sears and Coca-Cola, on the other hand, have
set out on what may be a long journey of strategic repositioning. Both
Coca-Cola and Sears are dominant in their core businesses. But Coke is
nowhere near dominant in the entertainment business it entered through
the acquisition of Columbia Industries. Nor are Sears's acquisitions of Dean
Witter and Coldwell Banker likely to be its last moves in developing a
leadership position in financial services. Both companies need complementary acquisitions, and perhaps even new business arenas, to create
balanced multi-business corporations. Diversification efforts so far are too
modest to move Sears significantly away from its dependence on retailing,
or Coca-Cola from soft drinks.

This is a dilemma faced by all diversifiers. A large core business gives
stability and permits gradual assimilation if new businesses are taken in
small bites. But incremental additions fail to make sufficient impact to
justify their undertaking, *if* the maturity of an existing business is what

---

*This was true of Textron prior to its acquisition of Avco — also a conglomerate — in 1985.

motivated a company to diversify in the first place. Having to choose between going forward or going back, companies tend to push ahead. In the process, flexible management of an evolving structure places demands on management that it is generally unprepared to meet and for which no uniform prescriptions exist.

Old conglomerates like FMC and Borg-Warner have developed organizational solutions of sorts merely by surviving. Strategy led. Structure followed. It wasn't planned; it evolved. Companies that didn't adapt, suffered. These "old" conglomerates are now spending more time retooling their administrative machinery and less time on grand strategy. Eventually, closer integration of businesses with even tighter corporate business relationships will be forged. It may not resemble the design of a GE, but it will certainly be more structured than the first stages of diversification.

First-time diversifiers are the most tentative in making organizational changes. Goodyear's 1983 acquisition of Celeron, a gas pipeline company, for example, allowed Goodyear to diversify away from its dependency on tires and presumably into a less cyclical business with more reliable cash flows. If these assumptions prevail, tires and pipelines can be managed as autonomous units. However, things don't always follow a script. The pipeline business may prove less stable in the future than was originally anticipated. Goodyear would then have to decide whether to manage it more actively by moving towards integrated controls, or admit its mistake and sell the business.

This juncture is eventually reached by many diversifying companies. Some have backed off. Armco, for instance, diversified away from steel, for obvious reasons, and into insurance and other financial services. Just a few years later, it had decided it couldn't manage the new businesses. The CEO of Armco explained, "My background is metallurgical engineering, like many of the managers here. A metallurgical engineer might know something about aerospace materials, for instance. But insurance and financial services? No."[2]

Armco couldn't — or wouldn't — adapt its management style to suit its strategy of unrelated diversification. Nor did it move organizationally from an initial holding company approach. As pure strategy, a diversified Armco may appear as a better alternative than an Armco remaining in steel. As a practical matter, Armco could not implement strategy because it could not manage two such disparate types of operations. And strategy without implementation is a sterile intellectual exercise.

Armco never attacked its diversification program in a total and comprehensive manner. It neither built on its distinctive competence in metallurgical engineering, nor pursued a gradual structural program of managing its acquisitions. Thus it was incapable of progressing beyond the first interim stage of diversification. In effect, Armco had only the synergy potential of moving resources into promising new businesses. When the prospects for these businesses collapsed, it was not prepared to manage them and it felt organizationally distant from the culture of insurance and other financial services. In the end, Armco decided to retreat to the cyclical nature of the steel business, even though the reasons for having left it in the first place remain as persuasive as ever.

Armco's predicament underlines the problems of moving rapidly into a number of new fields with neither strategic nor structural plans clearly in mind. At best, unrelated diversification is challenging. But without prep-aration, the odds against success rise dramatically. When change upsets the status quo, the ability to adjust to the changing conditions is all-important. For a diversifying company, this places a premium on the principles of *flexibility* and *differentiation;* that is, the flexibility to move in more than one direction, and the ability to differentiate among a company's various parts in order to be competitive in each major market.

THE PRINCIPLE OF FLEXIBILITY

Flexibility is the ability to manage two distinct types of grand strategy in a single organization. This duality is forced on companies that both acquire new businesses and grow from within. It is different from a purely com-petitive orientation to strategy. What flexibility implies, in short, is the ability to loosen or tighten headquarters' grip on operations as strategic positioning heats up or cools down. The holding company form of orga-nization is the most flexible because it gives the greatest autonomy to op-erations.

The holding company option is not a permanent solution, however. No company remains in flux indefinitely. Even a feverishly diversifying company like Beatrice must eventually pause and rationalize what it has acquired. When companies stabilize, either for relatively long periods be-tween bursts of diversification or as mature conglomerates, organizational reforms take hold. During extended periods of calm, companies transform organizationally to reflect past strategy and to prepare for the next strategic thrust. In a fully mature conglomerate, integration of the different businesses reflects a switch in emphasis towards efficiency of operations, in contrast to merely acquiring and divesting businesses.

Maturity doesn't mean a static strategy, or the total absence of restructuring. Stability is a relative condition. Organizations are dynamically changing as they evolve. Thus complete integration of operations serves as a continual goal rather than a point to be reached. GE comes closest to this ideal state in terms of being extremely diversified yet integrated along multi-divisional lines. The great majority of diversifying companies still are in transition. In these interim stages, companies must be prepared to move from stability to change, depending on the next strategic cycle. To achieve maximum synergy, both types of strategy must be managed well. In order to do that, the classic notion that integration is always the best alternative must be discarded. A rapidly changing company cannot be tightly controlled within a single unified structure.

The Role of the CEO vs. the COO

Integrated organizations exert authority from the top down. This is consistent with the concept of a single grand strategy for the corporation and all of its parts. Each level coordinates the activity of the level below and successively reviews, checks, and controls for the consistency of plans and strategies throughout the organization. The CEO and COO work in close proximity because they work in concert. Frequent communications serve to reinforce their common goals and a common set of strategies.

In a diversifying firm, resources are not all channeled back to the same businesses, nor does synergy depend solely on current businesses. The alternative to conventional design suggested in the following figure illustrates this dimension of flexibility.

The chief executive office and its staff is distinct from the chief operations office and its appropriate staff. This distinction can be underlined by placing each in different physical locations. Proximity is not an advantage when the tasks are sufficiently different: each office tends to be distracted and become involved with the duties of the other. Diversions are common, such as staff members grooming for their next move upwards rather than attending to specific functions. The operation of both offices would run more smoothly, and evaluations could be more objective and dispassionate without the intimacy now common between them. Technological advances in communications and transportation can reduce the loss of personal contact from working in different locations. What may be lost in direct contact can be compensated for by reinforcement of the distinction between de-

Traditional and Proposed Structures for Managing Unrelated Diversification

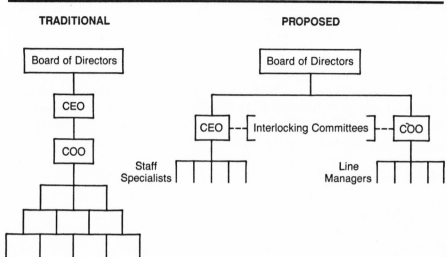

centralized and centralized management — a distinction that has long been recognized as sound in principle.

Finally, separating the two top offices also would make it easier to elevate or lower the relative position of the senior managers, depending on where the strategic emphasis lies. Conventional structures assume the CEO to be the top officer because his or hers is the highest point in a pyramidal arrangement. In a flexible design, the rewards and incentives can be more closely tailored to the major responsibilities for the bottom line. When the success of a company primarily depends on contributions from old-line businesses, then the COO deserves the authority and compensation commensurate with the importance of his or her duties. When the reverse is true, and the strategic emphasis is on developing a new mix of businesses, this places the responsibility for success of the company beyond the control of the chief operations officer.

In an integrated firm, chief executive officers and chief operations officers are both dedicated to maximizing performance through existing businesses. In these instances, senior managers' perspectives coincide. It is not uncommon in such companies for a single executive to assume both titles and sets of responsibilities, or for a second title, if used, to be largely honorary, as in an emeritus "chairman's" position. There is, in fact, no apparent bias towards the president's or chairman's title being used for the

CEO. There is little *strategic* significance that can be read into the choice by the top officer to be called president or chairman in a company where all jobs support a single grand strategy. For diversifying companies, the division in responsibilities may be better designated by chief corporate officer (CCO) and chief operations officer (COO).

In companies that engage in relatively long-term restructuring, the chief executive's office is too preoccupied with repositioning to contribute much to current operations in any event. Donald Kelley of Esmark, for example, was a numbers man responsible for the financial justification of each major acquisition or divestment. He was involved with the outside contacts — to lawyers, bankers, brokers, shareholders, and prospective new businesses — necessary for building a conglomerate. Little time remained to supervise operations actively, even if he was so inclined. Similarly, any diversifying company intent on doing a good job of strategic repositioning is unlikely to have a chief executive officer with the requisite skills (and time) to be a good strategic manager as well as a good operations manager. Failing to capture this distinction organizationally prevents a firm from making the best use of personnel.

Intimate collaboration between the two senior executives is a legacy of conventional organization. Where it applies, it should be implemented. Where it doesn't, companies will be frustrated by trying to bind two parts of the organization that need to be different. In such cases, corporate staffs overstep into operational strategy and line managers try to influence corporate level decisions. The first instance amounts to meddling, while the second abandons the corporate office to the vested interests of the different business managers. Form should follow function. This principle of architectural design also applies in the design of business organizations.

Both senior offices can coordinate with each other through interlocking committees, with supervision and direction from an active board of directors. A more participatory and professional board of directors is a desired objective in any case as companies become more complex and top decision-making power needs to be spread out. As conglomerates represent the extreme of organizational complexity, they also present the most forceful case for developing an informed working board of directors.

There is nothing magic or permanent about the current system. There are, on the other hand, well-recognized principles of motivation and reward that are impossible to implement satisfactorily in a diversifying company caught in an inflexible pyramidal structure. To obtain the inherent synergies from diversifying requires flexibility *at* the top and autonomy of operations *from* the top. In addition, a company needs differentiation among its various strategic groups of businesses.

THE PRINCIPLE OF DIFFERENTIATION

Flexibility divides a company in two vertically, so headquarters and operations can effectively pursue divergent sets of grand strategies. *Differentiation* creates horizontal separation among strategic business groups. Each group is designed to excel within its particular competitive arena. This accentuates differences among groups and reduces their common ties. It is also a means for forcing greater decentralization at the operating level.

The essence of strategic groupings is to assemble businesses together that are alike, and to distinguish them from other such groupings. In principle, each major group is a miniature business and therefore should have its individual structure, reward system, and style, all basic components of any organization. When integrated, an organization coalesces around a shared set of components. In an organization of several different businesses, unity within businesses is as important as unity across businesses. While some companies have gone part way in this direction, few if any have done it comprehensively. Most companies are still experimenting and reacting rather than designing their organizations to match their strategies. The sections that follow discuss the three components of structure, rewards and management style as they apply to strategic business groups.

Structure

IBM's structure allows for independent business units that are freed from customary corporate controls while their ideas are developed and tested. Tektronix established an internal venture-capital arm that sponsors and finances employees' projects and may take an equity interest in successful company spin-offs. Johnson & Johnson thrusts almost total responsibility on managers expected to take their ideas from start-up to production. Another firm gives its employees half a day each week for experimental research, as long as the work is related to their field. In each case, structure assists strategy. Innovation is fostered by shielding units from normal corporate routine and discipline. Whatever the technique, the hope is to instill risk-taking attitudes within a conventionally organized and bureaucratic firm.

In a diversifying firm the magnitude of the job is greater, but the task of combining different types of business units within an organization is similar. In both cases, structure can hinder or help. If properly designed, the different units will all possess a significant measure of autonomy. The diversified parent exerts minimum direct controls — mainly coordination of planning and financial functions — while most decisions are made by the respective heads of the discrete business units. The objective is to gain the advantage of smallness in a large corporation, cutting red tape and shortening response times. The importance of *true* decentralization can be illustrated by using Johnson & Johnson's managerial approach to its family of businesses.

Johnson & Johnson operates about 170 companies. This precludes its close supervision of each one. Companies are grouped into divisions, each with its own board. Divisions presidents are only one thin layer away from top management.

This degree of autonomy has served Johnson & Johnson well. It has successfully introduced many new pharmaceutical products and inventions. But the past success rate may be deceptive. Moving into the new field of medical technologies, Johnson & Johnson has seen its lead in computer-assisted-tomography (CAT) scanners taken by GE, and GE threatens to repeat with magnetic resonance (MR) machines, devices that give clear cross-sectional body images without the use of radiation. GE's chairman attributed the defeats to Johnson & Johnson's attempts to manage outside its sphere of expertise. "What pill people have done well in hardware, and what hardware people have done well in pills?" he asked.[3]

This is a surprising assessment from a chief executive whose company is among the most diversified in the world. A more plausible explanation lies not with Johnson & Johnson's range of diversification, but with how it was managed. A closer look at Johnson & Johnson's organization reveals that the aforementioned "thin" layer of management between the distinct divisions and Johnson & Johnson included a fourteen-member executive committee, virtually all of whose members were marketing-oriented and had been with the company at least eleven years. None had experience in the technology of medical equipment. No wonder Johnson & Johnson encountered trouble when it stepped outside the pharmaceutical business. While giving the appearance of a very diversified, very decentralized organization, it was actually designed to encourage only controlled innovation into businesses close to its realm of expertise.

The moral of Johnson & Johnson's story is to have a design in place geared to *where you want to go* rather than *where you've been*. If results depend on businesses with little in common, it is futile to manage these businesses with the same apparatus as if they were all alike.

This aspect of management was not lost on the Gould company when it reorganized into four key business groups in 1983. Each group had its own president and its own board. This allowed the appointment of working members to the board who had specific *business* skills, as opposed to corporate board members whose positions are often honorary rather than participatory. In a related move, Gould drastically cut its corporate staff in order to reduce the "oversight" of business strategy by corporate staff experts. Concurrently, the authority of group presidents was elevated by increasing their capital spending limit from $10,000 to $500,000, with operating boards able to give on-the-spot approvals. The groups also had more responsibility for planning and were virtually left alone by the corporate office. Although the CEO sat on all four business boards, he chaired none of them.

If there was a problem with Gould's approach, it may have been a swing *too* far in the direction of autonomy. Giving operating groups independence doesn't mean setting them adrift. The difference between a pure holding company and a truly decentralized company lies in the *intertwining* of unity and independence.

Having an overseer board for operations made up of each group president is one possibility for bonding the various businesses together. Groups need to feel part of the corporation. If research-and-development funds are partly centralized, for instance, the allocation decision could be a joint business-corporate one. A joint committee of business and corporate level executives whose principal duty is finding means of integrating across businesses is another possibility. There is no better assurance of success, in the end, than the desire of both levels to work together. This attitude can be fostered or discouraged by actions of the chief executive officer and the chief operations officer.

Schering A.G., a German chemical company, is an extreme example of organizational virtuosity. It has no chief executive officer. The company's six directors each have a specialty — marketing, finance, or technology — and each supervises an area of the firm's global business. This contradicts all management approaches known in the United States. American consultants have searched in vain for the "hidden" chief executive they feel must exist. The German directors make light of such apprehension. The system works because of tradition. The close-knit directors have been together for decades and have built mutual respect and trust in each others' judgments. At Schering A.G., things have worked this way for a very long time. Its stability allows an informal and collegial atmosphere to exist. Because consensual decision-making has been the rule, it is considered neither unusual nor remarkable by those who run the company.

Given a relatively familiar environment and an operations-oriented strategy, Schering A.G. might continue to operate in this fashion. In practice, however, Schering A.G. has found that this administrative approach works less well in the United States. To win the chemical business of large U.S. customers it must react quickly. Its consensus style often arrives at decisions too late for changing market conditions. In order to accommodate to the U.S. market, Schering A.G. introduced some modifications in organization plus some improved communications systems between the parent and its U.S. divisions. But it did not abandon its basic structure. An organization that operates almost automatically is a valuable asset. Unless the company decides to alter its strategy dramatically, or environmental pressures force it to change, Schering A.G. is an example of Darwin-like adaptation. It is not a model many firms could replicate. But given the company's heritage, it is a satisfactory solution in this particular case.

Prior to the 1950s, the single-mindedness of a Schering A.G. was typical of many large American firms, with the emphasis on building an inward-looking, integrated organization. With attention switching to conglomerate-style restructuring, divisional independence became a major new consideration. In companies like Schering A.G., it has no relevance. But for the many companies that have chosen diversity over relatedness and change over stability, new organizational innovations at the divisional level, as well as new linkages between divisions and headquarters, cannot be indefinitely postponed.

Rewards and Incentives

How people are rewarded has much to do with how productive they are. Ideally, the reward system keeps people loyal without making them complacent. A variety of incentives are available, including traditional ones like bonuses and stock options. Generally, these are tailored to business unit performance along some defined standard like return on net assets, as well as overall corporate results. In a traditional company, a uniform system filters down into the organization and spreads across it, rewarding performance in each strategic business unit.

In a conglomerate, rewards should encourage excellence in each business group. A second type of incentive should serve to promote corporatewide cooperation. Failure to take account of both types of rewards risks driving a wedge between business and corporate efforts. When United Artists was sold by Transamerica, for example, the decision was forced in part because of the unwillingness of the parent to devise special compensation for this business unit, and the chafing of United Artists's personnel under a system they felt had substantially shortchanged them relative to competitors in the motion-picture business. United Artists never performed exceptionally as part of Transamerica, partly because the creative business of making pictures was so different from the other unrelated pieces of Transamerica. These differences were never allowed to operate to their potential. In the end, the divorce was inevitable since neither partner seemed willing to bend toward the other.

An unwillingness or inability to acknowledge differences also led Tektronix's chief of operations to form an internal venture capital subsidiary. As an employee, he had seen his own pet projects killed because they didn't fit the company's long-range strategy. On becoming COO, he was determined to open up the company to innovative ideas. The venture-capital subsidiary offered a way to fund and reward those individuals who didn't want to follow conventional career paths. Selected venture managers now maintain their own budgets and make their own mistakes. The potential rewards for those in the venture-capital pool who succeed are as open as in any independent company with a good product.

This type of mixing and matching within the same corporate shell is what differentiation is all about. In a truly unrelated set of business groups, each group is sufficiently different to be treated separately, yet each one also has a broader corporate role as well. The tendency in many firms is to lean in one direction or the other.

One way to prevent such lopsided arrangements is to coordinate the various components of differentiation. In developing a structural component, for example, compensation could be the focus of a joint corporate-business committee. In this way, identification of problems and work towards joint solutions would reflect input from both sides. The important point once again is not to outline detailed remedies with general application, but rather to establish general guidelines to aid companies in developing their own particular solutions. Once started in the right direction, companies will tend to evolve structures, rewards, and management styles in accordance with their needs.

Management Style

The intangibles of organization can be as critical to corporate success as pure rationality. We have mentioned cases where culture and management style were incompatible with a planned strategy of unrelated diversification.

Granted that philosophy and style are important, perhaps even critical, the question, then, is whether this aspect of sound management must forever elude the conglomerate. What seems clear at this point is that if conglomerates are to be successful it will not be in a conventional way. In "excellent" companies, instilling the right managerial ethos depends on two criteria: (a) consistent adherence to a specific philosophy over a long period of time; and (b) a unifying philosophy that can bind the company together around a common theme. Neither concept is easily transferable to modern conglomerates. Because conglomerates are constructed by the assembling of unrelated businesses, it is unlikely that a common thread runs through each. What works in steel, for example, may be completely foreign to the financial services business. Thus National Steel's move into financial services had little common ground with its basic steel business. Steel serves industrial customers and emphasizes productive and operating efficiencies. The money business, on the other hand, deals with individual consumers, with the stress on service. Certainly, this situation contrasts sharply with the iteration of a simple philosophy like customer service or product quality that provides the drive in such well-managed companies as Hewlett-Packard, Boeing, IBM, etc., as chronicled by Peters and Waterman.

Even if this problem of unlike businesses could be overcome, the second principle of "excellent" companies would also militate against conglomerates. Assembled in a relatively brief space of time, conglomerates change organizational shape radically and frequently. Divisions are not viewed with the same permanence as a company devoted to a single business or closely related businesses. Thus, the time frame for pursuing a policy of "culture through osmosis" could not be duplicated by active diversifiers. The restructuring typical of active conglomerates would frustrate a typical top-down bonding of businesses over time by continually reinforcing an attribute they share or might jointly build on.

In sum, conventional synergy from a common culture or style is not appropriate for active conglomerates. This diminishes neither the importance of culture and style in certain types of companies, nor possible counteradvantages afforded by the conglomerate form. The argument that conglomerates *do* have synergies — although not of the conventional variety — is demonstrated by their continuing ability to compete.

Although conglomerates can't duplicate the approach to excellence pursued by integrated firms, they can improve the management of acquired companies with widely different styles and cultures. The key once again is found in achieving the right balance between independence and interdependence.

Heading each strategic group is a top executive with a role comparable to that of a corporation's top officer. And for each group, a culture identified with its particular blend of markets, products, and technology pertains. The trick is to use the common cultural ties applicable to particular groups as the basis for a cumulative synergy for the corporation as a whole. Gulf & Western, as an example, has stripped itself down to three main operating groups, with financial services as one of these three legs. In order to compete in the expanding and diversifying financial services arena, Gulf & Western is counting on its Associates subsidiary to lead the way. For example, in 1979 it purchased Fidelity National Bank in Concord, California, which provided a means for expansion of their credit card program and other financial services. Another, smaller part of its diverse financial services is insurance. All of these operations report to a single group executive. Part of this group executive's task, in addition to building strength in each business unit, is to consolidate and rationalize the various pieces of this strategic group. To gain the utmost advantage in this highly competitive field, the building of cultural synergy can be as critical to long-term success as operational interfaces.

American Express, by contrast, is a firm with tremendous operating clout and a visible consumer franchise in financial services, but it has had difficulty grouping and rationalizing several complementary acquisitions in this field. The American Express name and its established culture could not absorb the businesses it acquired without more attention than was given to the structural aspect of strategy.

Surrendering the corporate identity associated with a company's past success is not easy. It may, however, be temporarily necessary in becoming a successful diversified company. Brand identification is one means for maintaining an operating identity for various groups. It is logical for GE products to carry the General Electric name because the corporation is integrated throughout. For Beatrice, on the other hand, the attempt to identify Stiffel lamps, Culligan water products, Samsonite luggage and LaChoy food products as "Beatrice" — as the company tried to do in its advertising campaign for the 1984 Olympics — dilutes the importance of each product while failing to unify the family into a single image in consumers' minds. Beatrice is simply too diverse and changeable. It is premature to stress a single corporate image when facing at least several more years of evolution and change. As with the other components of organization, the timing and degree of adaptation should be consistent with the progress made towards maturity. Trying to force adaptation before its time can be as risky as not undertaking the necessary reforms at all. Keeping the balance between desired types of reform and their proper implementation is admittedly simpler to imagine as an abstract exercise than to execute. So far the attempts, either intellectual or practical, have been few and incomplete.

SOME REASONS FOR CHANGE
IN ORGANIZATIONAL DESIGN

Uncertainty is an unavoidable consequence of change. Moving to a higher stage of development can take decades, with many disruptive interludes. Because structure follows strategy and strategy itself may be impulsive, the perfect organization cannot be wholly designed in advance. The designs themselves are hardly ever permanent, and the more dynamic the company the greater the impact on structure. There must be leeway to accomodate such unexpected shifts in strategy. The reasons for change also need to be appreciated.

A *New CEO.* One of the likeliest reasons for new strategy is a new CEO. Chief executives are often reluctant to undo their mistakes, or admit they made them. New CEOs, on the other hand, often make their presence felt by major changes in their predecessor's strategy.

Upon taking the top post at ARCO, the new CEO William F. Kieschnick made it clear he didn't think much of the company's past attempts at diversification. Within a few years, he planned to sell all of the acquired metals and minerals operations except coal as well as the oil refining and marketing properties east of the Mississippi. Few big oil companies have been especially astute in their diversification programs outside of energy, but none have reversed course so emphatically as ARCO. Often described as a brilliant and imaginative thinker, Robert O. Anderson, the previous chief executive, was stylistically quite different from his successor. These contrasts are surfacing after his departure in the form of a new strategy oriented towards a slimmer organization more concentrated in the oil business.

A *Changing Environment.* Some decisions are made, others are forced. When General Motors decided to fundamentally rethink its strategy, it was responding to a growing market presence by the Japanese that it could no longer ignore. Without foreign competition, there is little reason to believe GM would have revamped its organization so thoroughly or so quickly. Also, there would have been less reason for GM to seek growth outside of the automobile industry by acquiring EDS, an electronics firm. In this instance, managerial decisions were significantly influenced by a rapidly changing environment for the domestic automobile manufacturers.

Changing technologies. Neither new chief executives nor reforms of basic strategy may be enough to protect firms whose products or services are becoming obsolete. Machine tool manufacturers, for example, currently face a crossroads. Smaller firms like Acme-Cleveland are having a tough time upgrading to a new technological state-of-the-art. Even big companies like Cincinnati Milacron are not finding the going easy. Automated factories of the future offer one of the best markets for new machine tools, but also involve dramatically new technologies and high costs of conversion. Moreover, machine tool technology is diffusing with the technology of such fields as computer-assisted design and robotics, areas in which old machine tool firms are running into formidable new domestic competitors, like GE, Westinghouse, and IBM, as well as foreign machine tool manufacturers. In the process of transformation, a whole industry may be absorbed by others, and assume a completely new dimension in the process.

Under static conditions, organization designs might be perfected. But things seldom stay the same. The more they change, the more impact they have on organization. By stressing flexibility and differentiation, structure becomes freer to follow strategy. In the face of continual strategic turmoil, no stable structure is possible. But as change moderates and companies seek stability, designing the "right" structure takes precedence.

Notes

1. Harold Geneen, "The Strategy of Diversification," in *Competitive Strategic Management.* Ed. Robert B. Lamb. Englewood Cliffs, N.J.: Prentice-Hall, 1984, p. 397.
2. *Wall Street Journal,* October 2, 1984, p. 33.
3. *Business Week,* May 5, 1984, p. 32.

5 HOW TO CULTIVATE A DISTINCTIVE COMPETENCE

C OMPANIES THAT STAY concentrated in an industry develop skills specific to that single business. *Specialization* is their secret.

Conglomerates operate in more than one business and rely on a breadth of operations and opportunities, rather than excellence in just one. *Scope* is the key for them.

Whether narrow specialization or broad scope applies in particular situations has never been a matter of serious study. Specialization has grabbed all the attention because it was the most traveled route to success. A firm producing a million shoes per year can do so at less cost per shoe than a firm that produces only 100,000 a year. The advantage lies in spreading the minimum costs of doing business over a greater number of units. In Adam Smith's classic pin factory example, the manufacture of pins was broken down into a number of simple, routine tasks. The specialized attention to each step allowed large-size operations to be efficient, and with increases in size indivisible expenses — like utilities and overhead — were lower for each unit produced. Adam Smith's notion of specialization as a way to gain economies of scale dates back to the middle of the eighteenth century. The question now is whether modern-day capitalists, like shoe-makers, should stick to their last.

KEEPING COMPETITION ALIVE

For an answer, one must ask why organizations are formed. Are ties to a core business a necessary part of an organization's purpose? Are organizations committed to a particular specialty, regardless of changes in industry conditions? Neither of these assumptions has been put forward as a reason for organizational structures. In general, a business is organized to maximize returns on resources invested in it. Litton has stated its mission more bluntly: "We are in the business of opportunity."

If optimum resource allocation is a fundamental reason for being, whatever restricts or prohibits achievement of this goal reduces its economic purpose. Capital must be free to move into and out of different products and markets. It is the threat of fresh competition that keeps firms striving to raise efficiency. If allowed protection from new competitors, firms located in a particular industry need only be as good as internal competition demands. Would the domestic automobile manufacturers have undertaken massive rebuilding and retooling programs to reduce costs, raise productivity, and improve quality without the Japanese automakers' deep penetration into their markets? Isn't the long-distance telephone business more efficient and less costly for phone users after deregulation? Hasn't wide-open competition in the computer industry — even with IBM's large market share — contributed to greater efficiency, with better products and consistently lower costs?

Industries tend to become concentrated, as we've seen, with a few large producers accounting for the majority share of business. Once established, the existing order is difficult to dislodge. Are small competitors going to knock off the big guys? Economies of scale set these odds as low. Are companies going to enter markets by building and organizing completely new businesses? Even theorists dismiss this alternative as too risky.

The best remaining option to keep companies honest and markets efficient is external entry, by foreign competitors in some cases and domestic diversifications in others. If outside firms have a distinctive competence that can be leveraged to advantage, they will threaten firms in every market not operating at peak efficiency. The continuing search for match-ups between competences and untapped synergy acts to shape the structure of industrial America. The difference in this generation from prior ones is that the action takes place without regard for the protective boundaries of a firm's industrial origin or from only domestic competitors.

The case for industrial restructuring rests on managers using their experience to gain entry into new markets, and their ability to carry out a strategic plan. Unfortunately, what seems clear in principle has been extremely difficult to execute. While the connection between competence and synergy seems a logical association to make, the record is littered with failures. Case after case attests to the need to keep emphasizing the importance of the basic fundamental principle: to cultivate a distinctive competence as part of the strategy of diversification.

Serendipity is not a Strategy

Skills have always been an important ingredient of success. But in the last quarter of this century, businesses will need ever sharper and more tailored skills for survival in more intense offensive and defensive encounters. The shifting of well-resourced firms from one market to another introduces new pressures and uncertainties into the familiar battlefields of competition. Vulnerable firms and underperformers become exposed and either create competitive advantages of their own or suffer the consequences. Depending on a haphazard approach to diversification, or defending against it, is not enough.

Nor is prior success in diversifying indicative of future performance. Smooth entry into one industry does not assure that a firm's skills will prove equally effective in other industries with different competitive conditions. After Philip Morris's success with Miller Beer, for example, it attempted a repeat in the soft drink field by purchasing Seven-Up. In this case, however, the strategy has yet to be justified. Seven-Up is at best a break-even proposition more than six years after the acquistion.

What went wrong? Two things seem clear. One, Philip Morris's marketing and promotional prowess did not give it the same distinctive advantage as it enjoyed in the beer industry. Coke and Pepsi not only dominate the soft drink industry, but they are equally proficient in the same consumer marketing skills as Philip Morris. Did Philip Morris perceive some other inefficiencies in the industry that were overlooked by Coke and Pepsi? The contrary seems to be the case. The key factor in attaining a large market share in the soft drink field is to penetrate the cola business that accounts for almost two-thirds of industry sales. Philip Morris must have had this goal in mind to justify the premium price and subsequent investments it has made in Seven-Up. But most bottlers of its Seven-Up soda also handle competing colas and are generally restricted by contracts from selling more than one cola in their territory. Thus they can't handle Philip Morris's cola product — Like — even though they bottle Seven-Up. Establishing an alternative bottling system would be expensive and risky. New bottling plants that would be controlled by Philip Morris could easily cost over $25 million apiece, while buying existing franchises means paying fancy price-earnings multiples, even if desirable operations could be found for purchase.

While Philip Morris has the resources to buy deeper into this market, it does so at the risk of ever-diminishing returns on its investment. Even as it develops its offensive strategy, moreover, Coke is busily consolidating and solidifying its own bottler network. For one thing, Coke has established large marketing groups whereby territories are enlarged and the fewer but bigger remaining bottlers reap the economies of scale.

The oversight of the key role played by distribution channels was a critical flaw in Philip Morris's strategy. Without a means for circumventing this roadblock, Philip Morris is faced with retaining what promises to be a long-term underperformer, or divesting itself of Seven-Up. In this situation, as opposed to the success of its Miller Beer acquisition, Philip Morris did not enjoy a clear distinctive competence, nor did it adequately comprehend the key factors for success in the soft drink business. If it had, it would not have entered in the first place, or would have developed a notion of how to overcome the bottling dilemma it now faces.

In contrast, when Philip Morris invaded the beer industry, it caught the major producers napping. It was allowed to build significant momentum before Anheuser-Busch and others retaliated. This fortuitous condition did not exist in soft drinks. Indeed, the soft drink market promises to become a battle of giants with the entry of Procter & Gamble (Crush International) and R. J. Reynolds (Canada Dry and Sunkist) in addition to Philip Morris.

The strategies of Reynolds and Procter, however, differ in important respects from that of Philip Morris. Reynolds's two acquisitions have large shares in the mixers and orange drink segments of the soft drink market. Each also has a strong distribution network to push these products through to the consumer. Procter must develop an entry strategy for mass cola production, and faces a distribution problem similar to Philip Morris's, but its approach is characteristically cautious. It is taking its time studying the manufacturing and marketing aspects of the soft drink business. It also wants to buy a small bottler in order to learn the distribution side of things. Contrary to Philip Morris, Procter & Gamble has limited its risk and exposure while probing for a competitive edge. Even if its efforts in the end go unrewarded, its investigative approach limits the potential losses and leaves less of the final outcome to chance.

Audit Your Strengths

Diversify from strength! This simple message, if consistently applied, could have prevented many of the early haphazard acquisitions by conglomerates. As mentioned earlier, the strategy of the first conglomerates relied on financial, rather than operating, synergies. Increasingly, however, the trend has shifted in favor of companies that have more to offer an acquired business than just money.

In some companies, the advantage being offered is obvious. Procter & Gamble, Philip Morris, Reynolds, Chesebrough-Pond's, and General Foods, for instance, are known as powerful and savvy marketers. It is their hallmark. Similarly, White Consolidated is fanatic about cutting costs and reducing overhead, a typical first move when acquiring a new business. Richardson-Vicks is a firm that has entered every new business segment outside its original Vicks cold care products line through acquisitions. An important criteria for their choice of targets has been to add to, or complement, an existing channel of distribution. Pantene, a hair care product, for example, gave Richardson-Vicks access to department stores and hair salons — two new distribution channels. Percogesic, an analgesics product, is sold strictly through drug stores — a channel that Richardson-Vicks likes to reinforce. In a similar vein, G. Heileman Brewing obtained rights to distribute a line of wine coolers — a mixture of lightly carbonated wine and fruit juice —with an eye toward using its 2,400 wholesaler network to give it a leg up on the competition in this new but rapidly growing segment of the wine business.

In each of the above cases, diversification begins with a sense of a potential strategic advantage. Synergy is possible because the acquiring company brings a distinctive competence or builds one. It still takes good execution to deliver the profits, but without this basis for a beginning the task would be immeasurably more difficult.

Admit Your Weaknesses

The flip side of emphasizing strengths is to avoid areas where the major strengths lie with the competition. Chances for long-term success diminish dramatically if a company has no expertise in the acquired business. In some instances, the best course is to admit a mistake and back off.

In Armco's case, for instance, facing the fact that a steel company made up of "metallurgical engineers" is unlikely to make a go of it in financial services may have prevented an even more costly mistake. Never prepared to manage the insurance companies it acquired, Armco decided to sidestep the onrush of new and powerful entrants into the new field of financial services. A number of other industrial hopefuls also divested financial acquisitions as the competition heated up, including Crown Central Petroleum, Greyhound, and Parker Pen. In each instance, these companies were not prepared to go the distance. With no particular strengths to apply to this new arena, these companies avoided what could have been a very punishing encounter as numerous giant firms maneuvered for advantage in this emerging market.

Admitting weakness, however, does not necessarily mean accepting defeat. Parker Pen, for example, realized it had little chance to survive in financial services and found an exit. It did, on the other hand, pursue its diversification strategy through the acquisition of Manpower, the world's largest temporary help corporation. This acquisition worked out very well. Manpower's performance kept Parker from a disastrous string of bad years in its basic writing business, and also provided an earnings base while Parker modernized its core facilities. In Manpower, Parker acquired a market leader and a company with excellent management, and thus a situation that could be operated autonomously until Parker learned the business.

The path Parker took worked out well in relation to what its fortunes would probably have been without Manpower. However, it is difficult, if not impossible, to foresee such successes. Venturing into a strange business without possessing any operating knowledge is risky. It is warranted only if the risks in the present business are bleak. It is, however, precisely in these types of situations, where unrelated diversification is the lesser of the risks, that companies often hesitate to act.

Armco's discouraging diversification into financial services apparently has numbed the company into reverting back to its basic steel business. Avowing to become a better steel maker, Armco is in effect denying that part of its strategy which showed this to be an untenable long-term position. By comparison, a competitor, National Intergroup (formerly National Steel) also acquired financial service companies, but only as a single move in an aggressive diversification program away from steel. First it cut the company's steelmaking capacity in half, and then it sold fifty percent of the remainder to Japan's Nippon Kokan K.K. Subsequently, National Intergroup sought to merge with Bergen Brunswig, a large drug distributor, and form a new company called Bergen National. If completed, Bergen Brunswig's shareholders would have the effective voting power to control the new company. The consequence could have been National Intergroup's eventual exit from,

or severe diminution of, its cyclical steel business. The strategy also envisioned the selling of its financial services and other businesses in order
to concentrate in distribution services. If successful, it would have been an
unparalleled transformation of a major old-line firm. Not only would National Intergroup have vacated the very risky steel business, but its management would have taken the innovative approach of letting another
management control the new company. Unexpectedly, at the last moment,
after the boards of both companies had approved the merger, Bergen Bruns-
swig's chairman cancelled the agreement.

National Intergroup's strategy was unprecedented, but then National's
precarious position in steel suggested an extreme remedy. The risks were
admittedly high. But so were the risks of remaining a large steel producer,
or imitating its competitor, Armco. By executing only half a strategy, Armco
has left its fortunes to the swings in steel. It may work, but not for the
right reasons. Every sign on the steel industry is blinking red. A few companies with technological strengths, or minimills serving specialized needs,
are prospering. But these are not the areas in which Armco's strengths lie.
Armco chose the risks it knows over the devils it fears. Even if successful,
this would be a defeat for strategic planning, signaling how little progress
has actually been made since the term came into vogue in the mid-1950s.

Admitting weakness is one of the most difficult aspects of a strategic
audit. Most companies emphasize their own strengths, and focus on the
weaknesses of their competitors. Yet only by facing up to one's own vul-
nerabilities can a company choose an optimum strategy. If properly exe-
cuted, such an analysis can be turned to a company's advantage. When
Richardson-Merrell decided to sell its ethical drug business to Dow Chemical, it did so while the business was still profitable and Richardson-Merrell
could exact a good price for itself and its shareowners. Both companies
benefited by the exchange; Richardson-Merrell by channeling former heavy
R&D expenditures into its remaining personal health care business and
Dow by adding a potential new business leg to lessen its reliance on basic
chemicals.

Searle is another situation where sale of the company was the desired
strategy. The Searle family, which owns over a third of the stock, was
seeking to diversify their financial investments. Additionally, Searle had
management problems and, except for the sweetener Aspartame, the company had gone through a long dry spell of new drug products.

If concluded, the sale would have enriched shareholders and probably
raised the managerial efficiency of Searle. Although the offer to sell was
withdrawn in 1985, because of an inability to come to terms, the reasons

for seeking the sale remain. Through the alchemy of diversification, the liabilities of Searle may still be turned into gold for its shareholders.

When initiated by management, the sale of an underperforming business is generally applauded. When similar results are achieved through acquisition, which also raises efficiency and rewards shareholders, the reception is often negative. One might question the objectivity of an analysis that gives sanction to one but not the other, when both produce the same desirable results.

THE IMPORTANCE OF MARKET POSITIONING

Corporate performance depends both on choosing the right businesses to manage and operating each business well. The effectiveness of market positioning in certain cases can be more critical than operational efficiency. Companies whose markets are undergoing drastic revision are the most affected by the positioning factor. Particularly vulnerable are firms that occupy segments of what are becoming larger consolidated markets. These companies are at the intersections of change and must decide which direction to take. In such situations, competitive arenas are being reshaped along strategic lines rather than traditional industry boundaries. ROI (return on investment) rather than SIC (standard industrial classifications) guides the restructuring process.

Three such examples of new multi-product, multi-service strategic sectors are office automation, factory automation, and financial services. In each, new competitors are upsetting the balance of old industries. Giant firms in once separate industries like electronics and office equipment; electrical/industrial equipment and machine tool manufacturers; and commercial banks and securities firms — to name a few — are bumping up against each other as several old specialties intersect to form broader consolidated markets of skills and services. For even giant firms to build a "critical" base of expertise in these new fields, acquisitions must play a role. Given the accelerated pace of technology, the time for creating competitive advantage is shrinking. The financial demands of restructuring also restrict the number of mass marketers to enter such new arenas. As in the evolution of every new business, an inevitable squeezing out will occur. For example, there were once more than 700 breweries in the United States; now there are fewer than 50. Only recently, commercial banks exceeded 14,000 in number. It is a near certainty that this number will shrink substantially by the end of this decade.

During these periods of industrial changeover, a considerable amount of corporate reshuffling takes place. Old businesses not fitting into new strategies are divested. New points of competitive interfacing are sought and existing ones strengthened. Acquisitions can add market shares, widen distribution channels, infuse managerial talent, and add low-cost capacity. This, at any rate, is the prospect of an efficiently functioning market.

Without acquisitions unrelated to core businesses, there is little chance for companies to achieve the desired degree of asset redistribution. And without such redistribution, consumers will be denied the efficiencies that such crossovers can bring. In short, it is the pursuit of old-fashioned economies. Only the scenarios are different. Economies of scale have been reached in most mature industries. Economies of scope are just now being thought of in strategic multi-business sectors.

The development of emerging new markets is the exotic edge of the industrial renaissance the U.S. is now undergoing. At the same time, companies further down the evolutionary scale also are improving their competitive positions. The pressure to seek economies by more effective regrouping of businesses is just as intense in traditional markets. Take the major appliance industry as an example. In 1945, there were some three hundred appliance manufacturers in the United States. Many were small, regional businesses specializing in one product area. Currently fewer than twenty firms make up the appliance industry, with the bulk of the market share belonging to six: General Electric, Whirlpool, White Consolidated, Raytheon, Magic Chef, and Maytag.

The trend has been toward a wider product line, with the largest producers now offering a complete line of home appliances. This movement to a "full product line" was a trend earlier described by Alfred Chandler in the evolution of big businesses in the 1920s and 1930s. At that time, the diversification into new product segments was internal. Currently it is accomplished through acquisitions, many of which are the divestments of large diversified firms. For example, Magic Chef purchased a refrigerator company from Rockwell International (Admiral) and a washer/dryer company from Borg-Warner (Norge). Raytheon had earlier acquired Amana refrigerators and Caloric ranges and in 1979 expanded into laundry equipment and dishwashers by acquiring two subsidiaries of McGraw-Edison (Speed Queen and Modern Maid). The following table gives a partial listing of the companies involved in this realignment of strengths and weaknesses through acquisitions.

Firms that lacked a distinctive competence in major appliances had no incentive for holding onto acquisitions made in this field. In a perfect

Who Bought Whom in the Appliance Industry

White Consolidated	Magic Chef
Acquisitions	Acquisitions
Hupp, 1967	Norge, 1979
Franklin, 1967	Admiral, 1979
Kelvinator, 1968	
Westinghouse, 1975	Raytheon
Philco, 1977	Acquisitions
Frigidaire, 1979	Amana, 1965
	Caloric, 1967
Rockwell	Speed Queen, 1979
Acquisitions	Modern Maid, 1979
Admiral, 1974	
Divestments	Carrier
Admiral, 1979	Acquisitions
	Jenn-Air, 1979
A.B. Electrolux	Divestments
Acquisitions	Jenn-Air, 1982
Tappan, 1979	
	Maytag
Whirlpool	Acquisitions
Acquisitions	Hardwick Stove, 1981
Kitchen Aid, 1985	Jenn-Air, 1982

world, the right match-ups would have been made the first time around. But if history demonstrates anything, it is the impermanence of a first strategy. Strategy is a continuous process. Some companies are further along than others, but none has run out of challenges. The unfilled agenda of firms short of their desired groupings of new businesses assures a continuation of the "urge to merge." In this new found flexibility of entry into and exit from markets, companies who expect yesterday's competitive conditions for success to be repeated need to reevaluate their thinking. They must develop new techniques, not only to seek out the conventional economies of their business, but to appreciate the early warning signals for change within that business.

In *In Search of Excellence,* an emphasis on excellence in what one does is the overriding message. It essentially pressed for building advantage by faithfully executing a few simple rules of management. Despite the usefulness of this approach for business managers preoccupied with day-to-day decisions, it does not address the basic issue of changing industry structures that is affecting a large percent of corporate America.

By clinging too closely to the book's central theme, a firm could be excellently managed until the day it files for bankruptcy. Mesta Machine, as previously mentioned, met the criteria for an excellent company, yet filed for bankruptcy in 1983. Given a new name, Mestek, the company was discharged from Chapter 11 proceedings in 1984. Required to sell assets to raise cash, Mestek emerged as a holding company with three basic units: Chester Engineers, a consulting group; MCC, a computer services firm; and Mesta Engineering Company, a 49-percent interest in a venture with the Pennsylvania Engineering Company.

Today, Mestek is a much smaller company than during its former days, when it supplied sixteen-inch guns to the navy during World War II. It also has veered away from its postwar businesses of manufacturing steel and industrial equipment. Treading cautiously, it has diversified away from cap-ital-intensive businesses, yet attempted to capitalize on engineering and technical skills. While still on uncertain footing, its new posture reflects the even higher risks of its former business. Had Mesta focused a little on the *changes* taking place in its industry rather than burrowing more deeply into it, it might have shifted gears much earlier and avoided bankruptcy court altogether.

A similar scenario making old business practices quickly obsolete is now faced by commercial banks, savings and loan associations, insurance companies, securities firms, investment bankers, and credit card companies. In each market, companies are threatened by a consolidation whereby complementary segments are being assembled into new conglomerates of financial services. In developing their counterstrategies, existing firms can-not continue business as usual, no matter how excellent such management might be. Excellence in conventional management while the whole market is restructuring is a euphemism for shortsightedness. Basic shifts in the way businesses are assembled and rationalized is a prevalent new strategic ele-ment in industry after industry. Yet this aspect of change is barely touched on by Peters and Waterman in *In Search of Excellence*. By hunkering down in a particular market segment, firms are presumed to excel by doing routine tasks well. This ostrichlike posture is strikingly similar to the classic eco-nomic ideas expressed in the 1920s.

The assumption of static industry structures has proven false, but the prescriptions live on. Faced with the choice between a familiar strategy and risky alternatives, many companies evidently prefer to wait for events to foist strategy upon them. In the presumably enlightened 1980s, progress in strategic management implies anticipation of the future and plans to create competitive advantage. It is a hallmark of the new wisdom. In actuality, much of the literature still contains old assumptions and old remedies. The possibility of raising performance by being in the right businesses is seldom acknowledged, although this is the single most important reason for industrial restructuring. It is also the means for companies to gain competitive advantage in the new structures that are being formed.

How to Measure Industrial Stability

When old structures begin to crumble, a means for detecting the signs of change is critical. Yet here, too, progress remains frozen. Analysis of factors which determined the likelihood of entry into an industry considered the industries themselves to be immutable. Even the recent revision of industry analysis introduced by Professor Michael Porter of Harvard relies heavily on standard methodology from industrial economics.[1] In its original formulation, entry into an industry was possible only if new capacity was created. Firms had to build their way in, according to the model. In Porter's revision, acquisition entry became a possibility, but it was still treated as an exception.

In the following table, Porter's five-factor model of industry structure determines an industry's average level of profitability and thus its attractiveness to potential new entrants. Deterrents to entry depend on various "barriers," such as economies of scale and absolute cost advantage. The higher the barriers, the less likely the threat of entry. Except for Porter's admission that "acquisition into an industry with intent to build market position should probably be viewed as entry even though no entirely new entity is created," the model stays close to the classical view. That is, the

Industry Structural Analysis from Industrial Economics

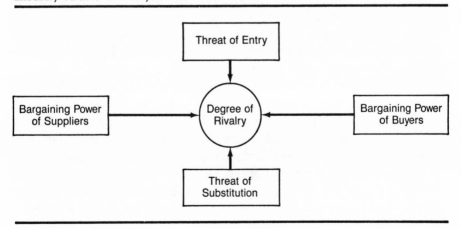

more barriers a company can create, the less likely it is that newcomers will penetrate its markets.

Once acquisition entry becomes not only possible but prevalent, this classic view of entry barriers collapses. For in fact, the very factors purporting to keep entrants out tend to *attract* acquirors. And if acquisitions are treated as equal and potent alternatives to building new capacity, they tend to overshadow the other four factors. To illustrate, let's look at the model's performance in several situations.

First, let's consider the auto rental business. From the perspective of the model, there are a number of barriers to easy entry. Once the choice airport locations are taken and economies of scale achieved, nationwide systems become difficult and expensive to duplicate. The model's vision of competitive analysis would alert Hertz to Avis and National Car Rental to Budget, but would be silent about the possibility or the desirability of each being acquired by a company not in the business.

Similarly, many of the major motion-picture producers have been acquired by large diversified firms — for a variety of reasons. During 1984 Walt Disney was the target of a number of takeover attempts. The model, as conventionally read, should have Disney in the catbird seat, since it has unquestioned dominance and production experience in its two major amusement centers, and an extensive library of unduplicatable films that bring in a steady stream of recurring revenues. These barriers serve as deterrents to competitors unable to reproduce these assets. If Disney were operated efficiently and the company's stock price reflected its true value, it also would deter entry through acquisition. If operated inefficiently, as some experts have observed, then Disney becomes a compelling target for takeover. The so-called barriers become responsible for a different kind of competition than the model envisioned.

Overall, the type of analysis in Porter's chart works best under static conditions, with companies competing on a common battleground with familiar challengers. What it tends to overlook is the inefficiencies within markets that invite acquisition offers, or underperforming assets that could be used to better advantage by someone outside the industry.

These overlooked aspects need to be considered alongside of Porter's version of the standard model of analysis borrowed from industrial economies. In combination, the two views can give a picture not only of likely changes from within but the prospects for radical change likely to be forced from without. In the following chart, a five-factor framework to evaluate the potential for such industrial restructuring is suggested. The five factors are:

Five Indicators of Potential for Industry Restructuring

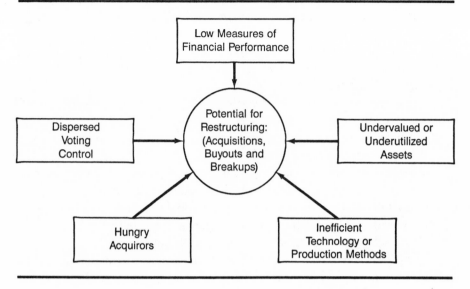

- Inefficient technology or operations
- Undervalued or underutilized assets
- Dispersion of voting control
- Low return on capital
- Hungry acquirors

Inefficient technology or operations. Falling behind in technology invites competitors to crowd in. The machine tool industry, for example, is currently being restructured by the entrance of new domestic competitors, as the technology of lasers and computer-assisted flexible manufacturing systems (FMS) demands greater skills than the old line tool firms possess. New foreign competitors, particularly from Japan, and the potential exit of machine toolers divested by conglomerates like Allied and Textron, also disturbs the status quo. The seeds for such restructuring were sown many years earlier, when the industry failed to invest to keep abreast of the new advances.

No longer can American manufacturers assume the edge in either the technology of products or the way they are manufactured. Our automobile makers borrowed from the Japanese their "just-in-time" inventory methods, quality circles for raising worker productivity, and statistical quality control systems. In a rush to catch up, General Motors has at least five Japanese partners in ventures ranging from robotics to subcompact car and truck manufacturing. In market after market, new entrants are challenging old leaders. Historical dominance in many cases has bred complacency and a culture resistant to change. In world markets where old methods are increasingly threatened by new approaches, failure to monitor the progress of others and invest in order to modernize can assure the displacement of once-great industry leaders.

Undervalued or underutilized assets. In July 1984, according to Standard & Poor's Corporation, nearly thirty percent of all industrial stocks listed on the New York Stock Exchange sold below tangible book value. When T. Boone Pickens of Mesa Petroleum made his bid to take over Gulf Oil, Gulf's stock was selling for 30 percent of asset value. All the giant oil mergers taking place around that time struck an average price equal to about two-thirds of asset value. Ironically, large conglomerates have themselves been viewed as likely targets for takeover and restructuring in order to realize a higher value from sale of the separate businesses.

Dispersed voting control. Acquisitions play a major role in industrial restructuring, and a crucial ingredient in an acquisition is obtaining the voting control to make it happen. Even giant companies have proven vulnerable where stockholdings have been widely distributed. Textron, for example, was the subject of a tender offer in 1984 by Chicago Pacific Corp., a company just a fraction of Textron's size but aided by the fact that directors and officers of Textron controlled less than one percent of the 36 million shares outstanding.

Complicating a defense from takeover is the concentration of shares in institutions that may be legally bound to accept an attractively priced offer. And over fifty percent of shares of large public companies can be controlled by pension fund and mutual fund managers. There are, as one pundit put it, no more loyal shareowners. In view of the small number of shares controlled by management and the subsequent vulnerability this spells for some companies, this factor becomes critical in an overall assessment of how radically or how quickly an industrial sector can be restructured.

Return on capital. A common invitation to entry is when firms fail to maximize the use of capital. When this underutilization persists, entrants will be attracted who either have the managerial capability to raise performance, or who may restructure operations in order to realize the underlying value. The reasons for underperformance may be due to technological or operational deficiencies, as noted above, or general mismanagement. This financial measure by itself gives no clues as to where the remedies lie, but it is often the trigger that leads to fundamental changes.

Hungry acquirors. A final part of the framework reflects the unpre-dictable and uncertain nature of major change. Despite all precautions and above-average performance, surprises can and do occur. For instance, large mature companies may be willing to dilute their earnings near term in order to establish positions in new and growing markets. They may "overpay" to gain entry, in other words, and undercut a purely rational analysis of ex-pectations. One business it is possible to envision for such a scenario is drugs. Companies like DuPont, Monsanto, and Dow Chemical are rumored to be seeking drug companies to buy in order to supplement their internal but modest thrusts into this market. Following historical precedent, Japa-nese drug manufacturers will eventually push to extend what are now mainly licensing agreements with U.S. drug firms into direct participation in the market through acquisitions of some of these licensors.

For many years, the drug companies relied on the difficulty of dupli-cating their operations as a sufficient barrier to entry. These same high barriers make acquisition entry the only feasible strategy. Meanwhile, the pressures for access keep building. At the same time the high prices of drug firms relative to all industrial shares has declined along with a drop in the productivity of R&D expenditures, further raising the potential for external entry and the possibility of major restructuring.

A Flexible Strategy is the Best Strategy

The message of the previous chart is a warning: *Don't assume industrial stability.* Continually question the assumptions of strategic entry and exit. The common model for structural analysis in Porter's chart on page 109 gives only a partial view of reality. In particular, it gives deceptive readings when relevant events occur outside the familiar industry setting.

Another problem with Porter's model is that one of the major ways to create entry barriers is to sink capital into large permanent structures not easily duplicated. This traditional route to economies of scale can also become a trap for companies seeking to exit from a market. Large integrated steel mills, for instance, are perfect examples of how to create high barriers to entry and equally big barriers to exit from later on. In a mature or static business, the past construction of high entry barriers could come to haunt firms that later seek to leave.

The undesirable effects of *any* barriers to entry or exit is the cornerstone of the previously mentioned theory of contestable markets. In no uncertain terms, it argues against the very barriers that the model on page 109 portrays as the basis for an industry being attractive.

Finally, the most important implication of the new analysis is the prime importance of reduction of barriers to entry. Certainly, all artificial barriers and particularly those which result from governmental intervention are put into question. Not only must firms be left free to enter an industry but they must be free to do so at the time and place they choose, without advance notice to regulators or anyone else. For otherwise the swift entry that takes advantage of an incumbent's misbehavior and which is the key to the power of contestability will be precluded."[2]

In sum, today's circumstances call for new methods of market analysis. Industries themselves are obsolete in the conventional sense. Similarly, the model for industry analysis is also inadequate for much of the industrial community it attempts to address. What is needed are measures of effectiveness for assembling new business groups as well as identifying inefficiencies that can be exploited in groups that currently exist.

The diagram in Chapter 3 (on page 61) is a general approach in this direction. It makes the alignment of synergies with distinctive types of competence the rationale for new strategic groupings. Coupling this insight with traditional structural analysis and suggesting where points of interface exist, for companies both inside or outside the market, gives a more comprehensive evaluation of competitive opportunities than a one-sided view of internally constructed markets.

TOWARDS A NEW INDUSTRIAL ORDER

Cultivating distinctive competences on which to base a strategy of diversification is part of the process of rationalizing conglomerate-style diversification. The postwar movement has seen professionally managed firms increasingly and systematically seeking competitive advantage. Acquisitions still don't always work out as planned, of course, and cases of clumsy execution are not hard to find. But two insights are worth making, since they have gone practically unnoticed.

First, a massive restructuring of the American economy is already in progress and observable in the erosion of old industry structures. Second, the tactics of diversification have matured along with the conglomerate movement. What has gotten lost by focusing only on the past failed cases of unrelated diversification is the many laudable combinations that strengthened competition. These wouldn't have been possible without the conglomerate trend. A few case histories serve to illustrate the point.

RCA's early diversifications followed no discernible pattern. The parent firm assembled an assorted grab bag of businesses, not untypical of the random collections of other early conglomerates. By the 1980s, after a number of top management changes, RCA decided on a new and more intelligible strategy. It remained widely diversified — into broadcasting, communications, and electronics — but it also jettisoned a number of businesses it had previously acquired and was never able to effectively manage. Invariably, these divestments went into stronger hands with a clearer distinctive competence for managing them, as in the following cases:

- Banquet Foods, a major poultry processor and frozen foods supplier, was sold to ConAgra, a diversified food company that already managed a large poultry processing business.
- CIT Financial was acquired by Manufacturers Hanover, a large commercial bank.
- Gibson, a greeting card company, was taken private in a leveraged buy-out.
- Hertz, a car rental firm, and Coronet Industries, a carpet manufacturer, are still part of RCA but logical targets for divestiture when the time and price are right.

RCA's divestitures meant a leaner and better company. Each divested unit made better sense as part of the company that acquired it. Economies were created on both sides. RCA now concentrates in those areas where it has some skills and experience, and is relieved of an enormous extra managerial burden. The new owners built stronger and more competitive business units. In total, the corporations, their shareholders, and the economy benefited from the changes.

Coke is also a large company in transition. Although not as diversified as RCA, it has acquired its share of underperforming businesses that never rose to their potential. Coke, meanwhile, shifted strategic gears. By acquiring Columbia Industries in 1983, it acquired a host of new businesses to cultivate. Correspondingly, the reasons for clinging to uninspiring old businesses became even more tenuous, and a process of redefining strategic groups included the following switches.

- Coke's wine business was sold to Seagram, which already had a sizable investment in wine that it wished to expand.
- Ronco Enterprises, a Coca-Cola unit that made and marketed pasta, was sold to Borden.
- Coke at the same time expressed a desire to move into the frozen-foods business and is looking for an acquisition in this field.

Underlying this series of moves by Coca-Cola is a strategy of leveraging strengths to get into new markets and avoiding those businesses where such strengths are not fully utilizable. Wine, for one, is a business that didn't meet Coke's criterion of relying on its trademarks, marketing expertise, or distribution systems to gain a competitive advantage. Selected segments of food, on the other hand, obviously appealed to Coke as fitting in with this basic strategem.

The Evolution of Strategic Groupings

Coca-Cola and RCA are only the tip of the iceberg. The amount of business swapping is broad and pervasive for a number of reasons. For one, a limited menu of acquisition candidates operating single businesses inhibits companies from following a preset pattern of growth by design. A company may not be able to acquire a single company in a clearly defined industry category, for example, because businesses that fit that description either don't exist or aren't for sale. The practicality of assembling conglomerates is that strategy must fit the available opportunities. With the trend towards unrelated diversification now more than three decades long, a certain amount of rationalization after an acquisition is made is becoming commonplace. For large companies in particular, it is one thing to plan the ideal acquisition, but difficult if not impossible to consummate such a "fit" in the marketplace.

Esmark, for instance, once shed of its fresh meat and energy operations, described itself as a food, chemical, and personal products company. As part of its continuing strategy of diversifying, it made an unsuccessful run at acquiring Stokley Van Camp and also purchased a minority interest in Purex. The company it wound up buying, however, was Norton Simon, itself a widely diversifying conglomerate.

In evaluating Norton Simon's potpourri of businesses, Esmark had to decide which pieces to keep and which to sell. Preliminary indications were that Hunt Wesson and another subsidiary that makes cans for Hunt Wesson products were the most logical retentions. Somerset, an importer of alcoholic beverages, and Avis, the car rental firm, were the most removed from Esmark's three existing strategic groups, to which Esmark would bring no special competence. Max Factor, the remaining large part of Norton Simon, was in-between, with some synergistic possibilities in combining with Esmark's International Playtex operation, but also a company with considerable management troubles. All in all, it was not exactly what Esmark had in mind for its next acquisition and clearly not a result that could have been forecast and wrapped into some kind of strategic plan. In a surprise finale Esmark itself was swallowed, setting off another round of sell-offs and strategic regroupings by Beatrice, the acquiror.

The specific outlines of strategic groups often are unclear until a specific acquisition is made. Moreover, the exact contours of strategic groups may be recast a number of times, as exemplified by conglomerates like Allied, RCA, Litton, American Can, AMF, and other companies evolving through several acquisition and divestment phases. This evolutionary process can take decades, with earlier acquisitions divested and new strategic concepts suggesting new strategic groups. In many such cases, the ensuing rationalization improves the structural alignment for all parties.

Entenmann's Bakery, for instance, was formerly a subsidiary of Warner-Lambert, a pharmaceutical company, until it was sold to General Foods. Would anyone doubt that this is a more workable affiliation? Ralston Purina's acquisition of Continental Baking, and ITT's sale of it, seem an eminently sensible switch. Surely Transamerica's sale of its relocation service to combine with Homequity, the relocation subsidiary of PHH, the acquiring firm, is a mating of naturals and a boost to competition in this market.

The pulse of the new industrial revolution still is to be taken — or noticed. Of the many books written on an "industrial renaissance," how many have mentioned conglomerates favorably? Most solutions for revitalizing industry lean toward government intervention or government incentives to make corporations do the right thing. None have commented positively on the most important marketplace alternative already at work: freedom of market entry and exit. It requires no new draconian policy or bureaucracy. Simple release of natural market forces is enough; that is, the freedom of enterprises to seek a legal profit, wherever it might lead. Properly channeled, the profit motive is more potent — and more effective — than all attempts at regulated solutions thus far.

Notes

1. Michael E. Porter, *Competitive Strategy*. New York: Free Press, 1980.
2. "Contestable Markets," *Wharton*, pp. 29 – 30.

6 THE ART OF CHOOSING STRATEGIC MANAGERS*

HOWARD JOHNSON was a pioneer in the fast-food business, yet McDonald's now dominates the field. Montgomery Ward and Sears were large retailers faced with the same options for growth after World War II, but Sears was the company that capitalized on its opportunities. Similarly, K mart and W.T. Grant saw their futures differently, the former developing a grand new strategy while the latter struggled from one unprofitable year to another until its ultimate bankruptcy.

Success or failure often relies on management's perceptions of its opportunities. In the above cases, these perceptions differed sharply. The differences in results couldn't be accounted for by a changing environment, since the firms were in the same industry faced with similar uncertainties. The results were the consequences of major strategic decisions. And such decisions were largely the responsibility of the firms' respective top managers.

As in the past, current decisions will prove some managements more insightful than others. It is logical, even obvious, to assume that good strategy depends on good managers. Without a manager's perception of a need for a change' in strategy, no change will occur. With an incorrect perception, the wrong strategy will be chosen. For firms diversifying into unrelated businesses, the correct selection of leaders is critical. And the most important task in manager selection is the choice of the top executive.

---

*Parts of this Chapter were taken from the author's article titled "Choosing the Right Manager to Fit the Strategy," *Journal of Business Strategy*, Fall 1982, pp. 58 – 69.

The head of a firm is its principal asset. He or she is the one who will set the overall strategic objectives and provide the leadership for attaining them. By choosing the right overall strategy, a chief executive can compensate for mistakes at less strategic levels. Viewed from the top down, the requirements for a good manager tend to be broad more than narrow, and intuitive rather than analytical. At the top, a chief executive deals with the highest level of uncertainty, encompassing all the strategy alternatives of the company's individual parts.

A MANAGER TO FIT EACH STRATEGY

The value of leadership hasn't gone unnoticed. Indeed, it is the hot topic of strategic management. The basic problem of selecting different types of managers for different tasks has been subject to microscopic investigation. The outpouring of suggestions differ in specifics but the substance is similar to managerial distinctions drawn earlier by others, including Max Weber, a sociologist; Joseph Schumpeter, an economist; James MacGregor Burns, a management theorist; and Carl Jung, a psychiatrist, who believed everyone belonged to a primary category of either thinker, feeler, sensor, or intuitor. The thinker is objective and thrives on facts; the feeler responds to emotions more than cold logic; the sensor acts instinctively and often reflexively; and the intuitor tends to be a visionary.

Psychologists belonging to the Freudian school of interpretation — like Abraham Zaleznik of Harvard — have drawn a simpler distinction between two primary types consisting of creative leaders and analytical managers. A colorful variety of subtypes have also been suggested by other writers. Common to all such classifications is an assumption that the psychological capacity for managing differs. Taking the right psycho-reading of strengths and weaknesses helps place the right manager in the right slot — a commonsense conclusion to draw. Yet plumbing the psyche is enormously difficult. Choosing the individual who is to be in charge often relies on a mixture of personal feelings and chemistry as well as factual review of a candidate's background and work history.

Andrew W. Mellon's experience, for example, led him to distrust engineers. In all his various business enterprises, he never once put an engineer in charge because they "deal with specific facts and with problems that always have specific solutions. . . . In business, however, the human element is very important. You never know what men are going to do. For this reason, engineers are not much use in handling business problems."[1]

Peter Drucker has said that "neither auditors nor lawyers understand much about business, nor do they usually have any people sense or any strategic sense."[2] Drucker's low opinion of professional types reflects what he sees as their specialized training and the rather narrow scope of their occupations. Such personal observations tend to overgeneralize, of course, but the point is that detailed descriptive models of managerial types overlook the subjective considerations in choosing a manager. The basic idea is to avoid selecting a corporal to do a general's job, and to be confident in knowing when a general is needed.

Three types of top managers are suggested; entrepreneurs, transitional managers, and operations managers. Each managerial type associates with the stages of diversified growth described in Chapter 4. Although these managerial types may seem close to those suggested by others, there is one significant difference. They address the needs of companies moving from single or related businesses to a strategy of unrelated diversification. It is this last change of strategy, the leap to a fundamentally different plane, that deserves special mention. The three management types involved in such a changeover are discussed below.

The Entrepreneur

Entrepreneurial managers are the antitheses of the professional bureaucrats. They create rather than manage, make bold new moves instead of cautious progress. Invariably, entrepreneurs possess strategic vision. They may have to energize companies grown accustomed to a comfortable managerial groove. Where inertia has had a long time to take hold, this requires heroic leadership powers and persistence.

In the first wave of conglomerate activity during the 1950s and 1960s, a brand-new type of conglomerate entrepreneur emerged. These leaders typically ran one-man shows. Self-confident enough to ignore tradition, they built sprawling enterprises from virtually a standing start. The Bluhdorns, Geneens, Ashes, Thorntons, Strichmans, and Lings were the captains of a new type of company, and their strong personalities elicited strong reactions. In the main, they were viewed with suspicion if not outright hostility. Their tenure drew comparisons to a new generation of "robber barons," a derisive connotation formerly reserved for the Rockefellers, Vanderbilts, Astors, Carnegies and the like. Over time, this perspective may mellow, as it has for their nineteenth-century counterparts. But it is too early yet to tell what lasting impression they will make on business history.

Following these one-man entrepreneurs of the postwar period was a more disciplined type of innovator in the 1970s and 1980s. As the strategy of unrelated diversification persisted, it increasingly spread to old-line, conservatively managed companies. These firms lacked a flamboyant or dictatorial leadership style. Nor did they attract the negative press and image of their predecessors. Their approach to change was more disciplined and therefore more acceptable. It evidently was credible to diversify away from clearly mature and cyclical businesses but outrageous to build an empire from scratch. The former approach reflected a different breed of entrepreneur — one who could work within an established tradition instead of flaunting the one that prevailed. Managerial routines build up over many decades in old-line firms presented different challenges and demanded a more participative type of manager. A Roberto Goizueta of Coca-Cola, for example, would never be called a "robber baron." Described as unassuming and even shy, he seemed at the time an unlikely successor to his predecessor, J. Paul Austin, who was seen as aloof or even autocratic. Once in charge, however, Mr. Goizueta moved boldly to change Coke's image as a powerful but sleepy competitor. In a number of uncharacteristic moves, Coke acquired and divested businesses like a born-again conglomerate, and Mr. Goizueta instilled an aggressive new spirit in the managers of its soft drink business as well. While Goizueta doesn't fit the image of the "robber baron" type of entrepreneur, there is no questioning the effectiveness of his entrepreneurial style.

A similar life-change is taking place at Sears. Long acknowledged as the king among retailers, Sears now has staked out several new markets for future growth. Edward R. Telling, like Goizeuta of Coke, undertook a formidable task with a style quite different from the 1960's entrepreneurial model. One of his initial strategic moves, for instance, was to form a four-person "Office of the Chairman," sharing his responsibilities and delegating power. Such power-sharing fit Sears's culture but would be inimical to a one-man style of operation. Despite the contrasts in styles, Sears was able to move fairly rapidly into several unfamiliar businesses. The methods, however, were methodical and thoughtful, contrasting with the almost compulsive buying sprees typical of the more free-wheeling conglomerates of the earlier postwar period.

In sum, the first conglomerate managers were "financial controllers," assembling numerous acquisitions in a wide and often wild array of businesses, based primarily on the bottom-line numbers. Later old-line acquirors, like Coke and Sears, could be called "strategic diversifiers," moving more cautiously from a solid core business and relying on strategic techniques and tools of analysis rather than quick instincts and a domineering style. A few financial controller types still exist, like Edward Hennessy of Allied Corporation, Dr. Henry Singleton of Teledyne, and Dr. Armand Hammer of Occidental, but they are in the minority. As the idea of unrelated diversification persists, it spreads to conservatively managed companies, ones in which the flamboyant entrepreneur contrasts with persuasive leaders who convince their top management team that change is the best of the available alternatives.

The Transitional Manager

Clearly, the job of succeeding an entrepreneurial CEO — especially of the dictatorial variety — is a critical but treacherous point in a company's long-term program of diversification. In this interim stage, accumulating the pieces of a diversified enterprise gives way to rationalizing and managing them. And a professional manager's skills become more important than those of the innovating entrepreneur. The transitional phase can span many years and several CEOs as a firm settles into a new style of management. Often complicating the situation is the lingering presence of an entrepreneurial leader who views with suspicion those who manage too differently from himself.

Consolidated Foods is a perfect case of the successor syndrome. Nathan Cummings built the company into the nation's fifth largest food processor. Succeeded in 1970 by William A. Buzick, Jr., Cummings never moved out of the executive suite. Although Buzick continued Cummings's diversification into nonfood areas such as furniture and apparel, Cummings forced Buzick's resignation in 1974. Part of the reason given was the break in dividend increases for the first time in nineteen years; but perhaps a simpler explanation was Cummings's reluctance to let go.

The next successor, John H. Bryan, sat more comfortably in the CEO's chair. Even though selling off many of the small, nonfood acquisitions that Cummings had bought, Bryan did not raise the ire of Cummings as had his predecessor, even though Bryan also acquired numerous food and nonfood businesses. Thus, Consolidated Foods's odyssey of diversification continues to unfold, even though significantly modified and restructured by the two transitional managers who followed Nathan Cummings.

Transitions from entrepreneurial to professional management are being faced by more firms as the original conglomerate-style entrepreneur dies or retires. How well or poorly a company passes this trial period determines its future and even its survival. In some cases, the random collection of businesses acquired by a financially oriented entrepreneur requires drastic surgery. If the readjustments are significant, the first transitional manager may be occupied with rounds of housecleaning before the traditional chores of professional management can begin.

When Charles Bluhdorn died of a heart attack in an airplane in 1983, Martin Davis took charge of Gulf & Western. Although a self-described professional manager, Davis's command after Bluhdorn's death demanded more toughness than professional skills. He fought off two notorious take-over artists who had minority interests in Gulf & Western, won the chief executive's title from the president of the company, who subsequently resigned, and moved his own management team up. Bluhdorn's beloved portfolio of investments in other companies were sold, along with many individual businesses he had acquired. While Bluhdorn would buy on instinct, following a logic only he understood, Davis sought a more reasoned approach to diversification. Although still widely diversified and still making acquisitions, Gulf & Western no longer makes acquisitions wholesale and purely on instinct, à la Charles Bluhdorn.

Quite a number of firms have had a first or second transitional manager by now, with mixed results. In the case of G & W and Consolidated Foods, considerable progress has been made even as the companies continue to diversify and evolve. Early conglomerates like ITT and LTV are having much bumpier transitions, while for others the transition has yet to start.

The specifications for a good transitional manager are fuzzier than either the entrepreneur or the operations-oriented manager. The stage of a company's development, how rapidly it evolves, the influence exerted by the entrepreneurial CEO, and how far the company still has to go in diversifying are all important factors influencing the type of person who should govern. Commonly, the transitional manager never attains the leadership stature, nor does he enjoy the unquestioned authority of his predecessor. Yet the difficulty of the task is often greater, requiring a blend of interpersonal skills and persuasiveness as the firm begins melding its set of businesses into a coherent single organization, at the same time that strong leadership is essential to keep the company moving towards its long term goals.

The Operations Manager

Very few companies have reached a position of relative stability in the sense of being as diversified as they wish and organizing effectively to manage that level of diversity. Among these few, General Electric is perhaps the model. It is an extremely diversified but strongly controlled corporation. While actively diversifying still, most of these acquisitions supplement existing businesses. An 1984 acquisition of a large reinsurance company from Texaco, for example, caused hardly a ripple in GE's management structure, although more than a $1 billion transaction. Having already a significant presence in industrial and commercial leasing, real estate financing, and related financial services, GE had the management structure in place to absorb this large new acquisition. An advantage of being a mature conglomerate is the capability of assimilating and managing such large new businesses into the existing management framework.

In effect, the entrepreneurial stage of growth for GE has long passed. GE began with a merger of three large electrical manufacturers in 1892. The railroad financier Henry Villard engineered this merger and, two years later, began negotiations on a second giant merger with Thomson-Houston, the largest company in the arc light business. Charles Coffin, the head of Thomson-Houston, became the chief executive of the new entity with the assistance of J. P. Morgan (whose investment banker firm financed the merger), who asked Villard to step down. Coffin immediately began to build the amalgamated enterprise into a single centralized structure.

By forsaking the practice of loosely controlled subsidiaries employed by other entrepreneurial firms of that time, GE developed a superior structure for effectively communicating and implementing a single strategic vision throughout all parts of this widespread organization. A second principal advantage was the use of internal managers and existing corporate strengths as the basis for diversifying into related or unrelated activities. From power generation, distribution equipment, and electric motors — its original electrical machinery businesses — GE expanded into turbines, appliances, and industrial controls, later into electrical insulation materials, then chemicals and metallurgical products, and subsequently into electronics, aircraft engines, nuclear power, and financial services. By continually evolving and refining its organizational structure along with its products and services diversification, GE became a uniquely diversified but integrated organization. By adapting structure to strategy, it maintained a central identity that most conglomerates lack.

Consistent with this unified structure, GE is now run by a strong "operations" manager, Jack Welch. With GE's current tremendous scope of diversification, Welch decided to concentrate on squeezing more performance from each existing business. Cutting sharply into staff overhead, particularly staff-level planners, Welch forced accountability down further into the organization, with the goal of being number one or two in every major business in which GE participates. Welch's approach is not easily copied by other diversified firms. First, he steps into a company already broadly diversified for a maximum spread of markets into which resources can be funneled and that also minimizes the risks of concentrating too narrowly into a single or few related product markets. Second, the culture and discipline of GE's organization is a major advantage in executing a consistent strategic theme throughout the corporation. GE already is a generation or more ahead of most diversified companies in these two respects. It may still not be the ultimate organization, since it has tended to diversify where its businesses led it, rather than where it planned to go. But in an imperfect world it is more perfect than the majority of diversified firms that compete with it.

SELECTION OF A CEO: TWO CASES

The personality of managers should be consistent with the strategies of the units they will lead. And of all the managers a company chooses, none is as important as the chief executive officer. The top executive makes things happen. Without a strong leader a company will make change slowly, if at all, despite all the strategic plans it might draft. Moreover, a powerful influence at the top can compensate for a weak system of strategic planning. "The planner, not the plan, makes the difference" is a truism that planners like to quote. And the top planner in any organization is its top officer. In the two cases that follow, an alignment between strategy and strategists in one company, and apparent happenstance in another, are illustrated.

The first case illuminates a strategy of corporate-wide revitalization at K mart and the choice of a chief executive to lead this strategy. After almost two decades of spectacular growth, K mart's progress had noticeably slowed, and competing discounters like Wal-Mart and Caldor were growing faster and more profitably than K mart. K mart's top management recognized the need for change. A new strategy was developed around an upgrading of the customer base — more middle- and upper-income customers — while concentrating at the same time on increasing efficiency, reducing costs, and broadening and improving the quality of the merchandise mix. The then CEO, Robert E. Dewar, a lawyer, made a rare admission by stating that he was not the man to lead the company in this new phase of development. "It seemed to me," he said, "we were at the point where it was very important to focus on the store." Rather than a staff man, K mart's rebirth demanded a person intimately involved with store operations.

The two most senior executives at K mart at the time were not selected, reportedly because the president, a veteran merchandiser, had argued against changing the formula that had worked so well in the past, while the vice-chairman, a real estate and financial expert, emphasized greater diversification and change than the final strategy reflected. Whatever the particular reasons, which are known only to the top managers themselves, another senior executive was selected from within the company. The new CEO, Bernard M. Fauber, was familiar with every aspect of the store, having started as a stockboy in a Kresge's store in 1941 at age eighteen, and having worked continuously for Kresge's and K mart since that time. Given the company's practice of promoting from within and its emphasis on remaining primarily a discounter, the selection of Bernard M. Fauber as CEO seems a logical association between strategy and management style.

The second case concerns the DuPont Corporation. In 1981, DuPont elected a CEO and a chief operating officer (COO). Both men had strikingly similar backgrounds. Each was a chemist who had a long career at DuPont. They were colleagues in the plastics department and later served on the executive committee of the company. They see themselves as complementing one another, with the CEO having experience in research, manufacturing, and general management, while the COO has a background in marketing, pricing, and plant start-up. In a broad strategy context, both men were expected to lead DuPont along a fairly familiar path for future growth: diversifying into specialty products, especially products involving the biosciences, but staying essentially a dominant chemical producer.

This was the apparent strategy until the opportunity to purchase Conoco, the nation's eighth largest oil company, came along in mid-1981. This was a fortuitous opportunity. Anxious to escape acquisition by Seagram, Conoco's management voted to accept an acquisition agreement worked out with DuPont. The final merger created a giant diversified organization. The question is whether DuPont is capable of handling the organizational problems and opportunities such diversity creates. It was not the result of planned strategy. In that sense, DuPont is not as prepared as if the merger was a conscious diversification move. Moreover, the selection of the top people to run DuPont was consistent with an earlier strategy of continued emphasis on the chemical business with a constrained strategy of closely related diversification.

Will DuPont's management team be equally adept at running a diverse and complex structure created by the combination of two giant firms in different industries? If the basic premise of selecting managers to fit strategies is correct, the present accomodation is basically a holding pattern. According to previous combinations of this pattern, Conoco will be operated as an independent business until a change in DuPont's top team maps a clearer set of diversification guidelines and decides what corporate role Conoco is going to play.

Although a successful fit is never assured — i.e., good managers may be the victims of random disasters and unpredictable environments — the odds favor structure over pure chance. In our two cases, the odds lean toward the structured approach of K mart, where selection was consistent with its strategy of remaining a dominant retailer. DuPont's move, on the other hand, was inconsistent with its long-term strategic intention of remaining in the chemical business, and also with a steady-state management style reflected in its choice of top executive officers.

PREPARING MANAGERS
FOR THE CHIEF EXECUTIVE'S POSITION

Given that the right manager can make a difference, can a manager be "prepared" for the top job? Is there special training that hasn't been tried, or widely applied, in gearing an executive to handle the difficult task of managing a company going in new directions? The rotation of executives among various top posts within a firm is common enough, of course, but this primarily gives a feel for running existing operations rather than managing a new type of organization. In a steady-state environment, where a firm contemplates no major restructuring, this approach need cause no strategic waves. In a rapidly evolving firm, however, change is endemic and past routine is inadequate preparation for coping with it. A suggested innovation in such cases is to choose the new CEO well in advance of his or her taking office; giving adequate time for developing a strategy for the firm he or she will soon lead. Once in office, everyday pressures tend to consume all available time. For this important decision in a dynamic company, doesn't it make sense to give the new leader time to formulate the best strategy?

Such a deliberate procedure was tried at two firms, both of which afterwards performed brilliantly. As in all prescriptive advice, no future guarantees apply. But the stories of Harry Cunningham of K mart and Donald Kelley of Esmark provide two examples of success worth considering.

Cunningham's entry into the top position at K mart (called the S. S. Kresge Co. then) was not a masterpiece of planned execution. The story has it that the prior chief executive didn't want Cunningham around the office. Cunningham himself suggested travel as an alternative to hanging around corporate headquarters. "I had no mandate," said Cunningham, "I was simply turned loose." In an impressionistic encounter, he met Eugene Ferkauf who had had just opened an E. J. Korvette store on Long Island, a new model for discount stores at that time. Spending an entire day there, Cunningham talked to buyers, salespeople, customers — anyone who would listen to him. He came away impressed with the basic discount concept: a free-standing store in the suburbs with plenty of parking space. The margins would be kept low, helped by customer self-service, open-rack displays and strong advertising support. The key ingredient for Cunningham was "that every item must move — turnover, turnover, turnover."

Determined from this and other experiences that discounting was the way to go, Cunningham kept his own counsel at first. At the time, discounting was not respectable. Even after becoming CEO, Cunningham made no immediate sweeping changes. Even though he had the authority, Cunningham realized that "if you haven't sold the people in your organizations, you'll fall flat on your face." He had to convince them they had an important part to play in this new venture. Also, Cunningham's enthusiasm and charisma were no small help in selling the idea.

In the end, Cunningham succeeded in innovating a new and formerly suspect discounting strategy. He cut prices, insisted on good value for the money, stressed customer service and a clean and orderly store. Each store was standardized in size and central merchandising policies but, within that context, store managers were given latitude in running their operations.

Cunningham's leadership style may have made him a successful chief executive even without the K mart concept. But without the time off to reflect and develop an idea of what he wanted to do as CEO, he would not have been as prepared or as innovative. One reason this story played out so well is because the chief actor learned his part before being asked to perform. Having strong ideas of what to do, he was able to concentrate on the equally important aspect of execution, persuading others to help implement his vision.

Don Kelley spent a similar period preparing for his succession, albeit for a very different kind of company. Kelley was and is foremost a numbers man. He is the classic "financial controller" type of entrepreneur. His promotion, like Cunningham's, was probably assured by his innate management genius. But also like Cunningham he was undoubtedly helped by the opportunity to intensively study the organization he was later to head.

In the mid-sixties, conglomerates were busily acquiring businesses of all kinds. One chief executive who was determined not to be taken over was the chairman of Swift, the old-line meat packer. He sent Kelley, then the controller, on an exhaustive review of the company's situation and alternatives. It was, according to Kelley, a "painstaking, nine-month, seven-day-a-week, thirty-six-hour-a-day" assignment.

He evidently learned what he needed to know. From his analysis, Swift transformed itself into Esmark, a holding company with Swift as a meat-packing division. In 1977, Kelley became CEO of Esmark. The rest is history. Donald Kelley succeeded in restructuring Esmark away from oil and chemicals and much of the meat-packing business, and into consumer products like International Playtex; eventually acquiring Norton Simon, itself a diversified consumer goods business; and finally selling Esmark to Beatrice at a fancy price. Not at all similar to what Cunningham did for Kresge. But in one respect both CEOs were alike. They both hit the floor running, aided by a clear idea of where they wanted to go and given the opportunity and exposure to know best how to get the job done. This may not be the perfect solution in all cases, but it is clearly better than muddling through. To quote Lyman Hamilton, a former CEO of ITT, "Every CEO says he plans for a long term. But every CEO lies."

Two Factors to Consider in Choosing the Right Manager to be CEO

Who Decides. In choosing a new CEO, who decides obviously influences the type of person who gets picked. If the outgoing chief is particularly strong, he may make the choice. Such selections may not be made for the right strategic reasons and often wind up to be personal miscalculations as well. The situations of strong-willed chief executives and shortlived successors is commonplace, involving such strong personalities as Geneen (ITT), Paley (CBS), Cummings (Consolidated Foods), and Trautman (Greyhound). It is partly a case of a once-domineering CEO exercising his whim plus a pliant management team and board of directors unwilling to contradict his choice. But a strong-willed or "entrepreneurial" CEO generally is in a poor position to choose a successor objectively. Top executives tend to pick people who reflect the qualifications they most admire. But an entrepreneur's skills are not generally the qualifications his successor needs. Companies change. Qualifications change. What an outgoing CEO often seeks are personal traits that mirror his own, which may or may not complement the new strategic needs of the firm.

When the board of directors makes the choice, the decision is subject to random variables as well. It seldom has extended contact with the candidates in line for the CEO's position. The board itself may be split, with internal factions dividing along personal lines that have little to do with the candidate's qualifications. Where boards are strong, well-informed, and hardworking, they are the most objective and logical source for choosing new chief executives. In too many instances, however, the members of boards of directors serve for reasons other than competence and ability. A casual reading of the membership of large companies reveals an incestuous relationship among the members and their interests as lawyers, consultants, and financial advisors. By the same token, cronyism among a company's top officers and presumably independent directors too often prevails. In such cases, the formal theory of managerial selection gets derailed by the practical imperfections of the system.

An informative insight on this score was given by Lee Iaccoca in the chronicle of his experiences after taking the reins at Chrysler. Although Chrysler had been led by former accountants, this expertise apparently wasn't applied to Chrysler's financial system. According to Iaccoca, financial controls were almost nonexistent. "I couldn't find out *anything*. This was probably the greatest jolt I've ever had in my business career." Similar disasters were uncovered in such areas as inventory controls, dealer relations, and product quality. As for the board of directors, Iaccoca could only wonder where they were when all of this was going on. He was not so impolitic as to accuse those who had just hired him. But once or twice he did ask, as politely as he could: "How did management ever get their plans past such a distinguished group of businessmen? Didn't you guys get any information?"[3]

What Are the Criteria? Assuming integrity in those who choose the chief executive, are the right criteria being used? It depends. To spot up-and-comers, many companies rely on internal identification programs and psychological tests. A proliferation in the numbers of industrial psychologists reflects an increased dependence on such testing. And psychological evaluations can be very useful. They help avoid a disastrous choice when a person's surface charm breaks under the stress and cross-checking of a four-and-a-half-hour psychological test. Several companies have developed extensive data banks from such tests that show critical associations between managers' characteristics and management functions, giving guidelines for important signs to look for when hiring a new executive.

The idea of testing for aptitude is hardly new. AT&T pioneered its application to industry in the 1930s. AT&T also claims to have an abundance of data to verify its ability to spot the fast movers. Similarly, other large companies have tests tailored for evaluating their rising stars, with similar convictions of their usefulness. Such tests, however, are applicable primarily for middle-level managers. As managers escalate up the corporate ladder, reliance shifts over to personal evaluations and chemistry, and the right background.

There is another important difference. Whether a person is promoted from within or is recruited, previous experience is generally the strongest qualification for promotion. This works up to a point. As long as the last job is like the next, a similar pattern for promotion can be used. As long as a company stays its course, for instance, an operations-type manager can continue to fit the bill. It is when companies change that the selection of a new CEO is most critical, and it is precisely at this juncture that relying on conventional practices is risky. Planning for change in a diversifying company requires a creative and strategic grasp for opportunities. In organizational jargon, an "organic" style is demanded. But the common approach to promotion often "rewards" a tough line manager by giving him the ultimate staff job. While an operations background trains one to deal with problems in a straight-ahead manner, a CEO's responsibilities demand a generalist able to think laterally. The ensuing force-fit produces a conscientious but ineffective effort by the new CEO to switch roles — from thinking tough to thinking big. In such cases, the firm risks losing an excellent tactical executive and gaining a poor strategic leader. It represents the proverbial square peg trying to fit into a round hole.

One way to avoid the most obvious of such mismatches is to first break down the routine of the CEO's position in general terms, like outside contacts, image-building, internal communications, and decision-making. Do these tasks fit the character, background, and personality of the candidate? Surprisingly, such inspection of what the chief executive is supposed to do, in a carefully defined pattern of duties, is seldom used as a guide in determining the fit of persons being considered to step into the CEO's shoes. In addition, the strategic path the company is expected to travel in the next three to five years should be an important guide to the selection process. These two dimensions to a CEO's position tower above all others but are not always the lead or even secondary criteria in making the final decision.

A CLASH OF CULTURES

There is no known defense against incompatibility, whether between top executives or between two companies. When Joseph Freeman assumed the top office at AM International in 1983, it was a very troubled company just emerging from a Chapter 11 bankruptcy. From nine consecutive quarters in the red, Joe Freeman brought the firm into the black. He cut costs, arranged more favorable credit terms, and worked hard to raise sales. Evidently he didn't spend enough time in another direction — keeping his board of directors happy. They ousted him after seventeen months on the job and a successful turnaround. No overt reasons were given, but it was speculated that Freeman was better with numbers than with people. Internal sources cited the need for someone with better marketing and strategic skills.

At Standard Brands, Reuben Gutoff, a long-range strategist who had worked at GE, was fired after only seventeen months as president. Here again, it was style that mattered most in the end. A thirty-year veteran at Standard Brands succeeded Gutoff and returned the company to its traditional operations-based focus and emphasis on day-to-day details and execution.

In the case of a merger of unlike businesses, strained personal relations at the top are not uncommon. The reasons for stress are many. Contrasting personalities can clash, or one executive dominates the other, or one company accounts for most of the profits, or an entrepreneurial firm is acquired by a conservatively managed company. All are common afflictions between marriages of contrasting business partners.

The body count tends to rise as conglomerate-style activity intensifies. In 1981, to give a single example, Phibro Corp., an international commodities trader, bought Salomon Brothers, a successful securities firm, to form Phibro-Salomon. The firm initially was set up as a holding company, with two assertive and independent parts. Before the merger, the securities side of the company had languished, while Phibro benefited from price inflation and resulting large price swings — and profits — in its commodities business. After the merger, the two businesses reversed courses. Buoyed by a boom in securities' volume, Salomon's executives became increasingly restive as they began carrying the now-limping commodities business. A fiercely competitive and combative top executive at Salomon eventually won the battle for heading the entire organization. In the end, the turn in fortunes between the two companies, aided by the personal style of Salomon's chief, made a fight for supremacy unavoidable. In turn, the rationale for the combination now may unwind. Seen from the new CEO's perspective, Salomon gave much more than it got. While Phibro's overseas contacts could aid Salomon, the new CEO doesn't see "how we [Salomon] can be of help to them " Without a better perception on synergy, it may be only a matter of time before the new CEO tries some drastic surgery.

Whenever a company ventures into a business it either doesn't understand or care to get to know better, trouble is not far behind. Oil companies as a group were tentative in their nonenergy acquisitions from the start. Mobil's purchase of Marcor, Standard Oil of California's minority interest in American Metal Climax, Standard Oil of Indiana's buyout of Cyprus Mines, ARCO's acquisition of Anaconda, and Exxon's acquisition of Reliance Electric probably would not be repeated today. After a flurry of interest in diversification, oil companies now prefer to stay close to familiar surroundings. The cultural aspects of new businesses just didn't take, not necessarily because of fundamental flaws in the strategies but because of an entrenched and inflexible "oil-man's" style that made long-term coexistence unlikely. Under such circumstances each cyclical downturn provided an excuse to undo a strategy that was never firmly committed to in the first place.

CHIEF EXECUTIVES WHO WON'T RETIRE

In most organizations, retirement is mandatory at a certain age. In business, the CEO may be the exception. Unless they are forced out, the attraction of power persuades dominant executives to stay. These executives make their own rules and set their own timetables, sometimes vowing to stay until their plans are carried out. The influence of a long and sometimes suffocating tenure at the top tends to stifle capable successors and leave a thin layer of good middle managers.

This raises several predicaments for a company. First, when the CEO vacates can the vacuum suddenly be filled without ungroomed successors? Second, the strategy of such a company is what the CEO wanted it to be, with the consequence that a new CEO has no clear guidelines to follow nor the "entrepreneurial" personality to imitate his predecessor. Finally, as previously noted, CEOs who retire but won't let go disrupt the transition to a new chain of command — and progress on major reforms or revisions of obsolete policies. (In the following table, some leading executives of this caliber are listed.) Without these entrepreneurial leaders stepping down, the evolution towards more professional management is postponed. Also, the next manager may inherit an ossified or atrophied management structure.

A variation on this practice is the founding family that clings to control but lacks the necessary managerial training. The switch from owner-managers to professional management has occurred long ago in most large firms. Companies like Norton and Stone Container have made relatively recent

**Conglomerate-Style Entrepreneurs
Who Are Still at the Helm in 1984**

COMPANY	CHIEF EXECUTIVE OFFICER
Allegheny International	Robert J. Buckley
Allied Corporation	Edward L. Hennessy
City Investing	George F. Scharffenberger
Colt Industries	George Strichman
Figgie International	H. E. Figgie, Jr.
Fuqua Industries	J. B. Fuqua
W. R. Grace	Peter Grace
Kidde	Fred R. Sullivan
Northwest Industries	Ben W. Heineman
Occidental Petroleum	Dr. Armand Hammer
Ogden	Ralph E. Ablon
Teledyne	Dr. Henry E. Singleton
United Technologies	Harry Gray

and smooth transitions to nonfamily chief executives. Hallmark also is a newcomer to this changeover in the top ranks of management. Its new executive vice-president, Irv Hockaday, is the first senior executive who is neither a longtime employee nor a member of the founding Hall family. With authority for acquisitions, Hockaday is wasting no time guiding this venerable privately controlled company into such new fields as specialty publishing, crayons, and broadcasting — with hints at future diversification into such unrelated businesses as insurance and computer software.

There is no particular advantage or virtue of a professional manager over an owner-manager. Having a professional manager in charge does not guarantee a superior strategy. It is, however, an inevitable stage in a corporation's development. Companies that prepare for that eventuality make the best transitions. Those that don't can leave their companies exposed to a period of wrenching adjustments as the firm prepares for competitive battles with a management team ill-equipped to defend itself.

Notes

1. *Wall Street Journal*, August 29, 1980, quoting from Burton Hersch, *The Mellon Family*. New York: Morrow Press, 1978.
2. "Conversation with Peter F. Drucker," *Organizational Dynamics*, Spring 1974, p. 49.
3. Lee Iaccoca, with William Novak, *Iaccoca: An Autobiography*. New York: Bantam, 1984.

Part Three

THE BUILDING
CHALLENGE

7 PLANNING FOR CHANGE

S TRATEGY BEGETS STRUCTURE. As companies evolve, managements adjust.

Strategy also involves plans. Stable environments place the fewest demands on planning. Even large companies, if concentrated in a single industry and following a long-standing grand strategy, tend to employ a standard planning routine. For companies diversifying into unrelated businesses, on the other hand, the complexity of planning rises dramatically.

In the conglomerate case, planning is stretched as never before. The always difficult decision of allocating scarce resources is compounded by the risks and rewards involved in external investments. Diversifying companies also can and do divest businesses. Selling off divisions has become as common to conglomerate strategy as mergers and acquisitions. The variations on strategy that conglomerates generate make the planning job infinitely demanding.

The need for planning to accomodate strategy is clear. What is equally clear, but seldom made explicit, is the need for more than one system of planning to accommodate radically different types of strategy. The problem of unrelated diversification is how to go from planning geared to a tightly integrated organization to planning in a loose administrative structure of conglomerate parts.

Surely the planning system good for one era cannot be copied by companies pursuing completely different missions. It seems unlikely, for example, that Consolidated Foods could be adequately served with the same planning fundamentals that satisfy the J. M. Smucker Company, even if both companies are classified as "food" businesses. While Consolidated Foods has actively acquired and divested companies, and then acquired and divested some more, Smucker has been content to solidify its position as the leading company in its relatively narrow niche of the multi-billion-dollar food business. The missing link in the planning literature is the difference between planning for a Consolidated Foods and planning for a company like Smucker.

To use a military analogy, companies diversifying into unrelated businesses require bold strategic initiatives as well as methodical tactics to wear the enemy down. This means honing a new set of skills: i.e., positioning the firm in the right markets, determining the optimum mix of businesses, and allocating resources among different businesses. Strategic positioning has planning implications different from the traditional practices for gaining market share and raising profit margins. It also shifts emphasis to corporate-wide planning supervised by the chief executive, separate and apart from business plans developed by line management. As in conducting battle, the commander-in-chief guides overall strategy apart from the field commander. Both jobs are important — and neither substitutes for the other.

THE PROBLEMS WITH PLANNING TODAY

How to design plans to best competitors has always been a top corporate priority. Since the mid-1950s, a number of technical tools and a new breed of staff experts have contributed to the formality and sophistication of how companies plan. Add to this the thousands of management consultants, and a large workforce emerges that is dedicated to what is today called "strategic planning." Amid this intensity, however, the feedback on strategic planning shows misgivings. A survey by Booz, Allen & Hamilton of firms represented in a *Business Week* conference on planning found that "80 percent of the 145 participating firms indicated that they were dissatisfied with the poor results of their strategic planning."[1]

Although the commitment to planning remains strong, comments like the one above suggest a sobering of expectations. Managements that embraced planning enthusiastically at first and almost without reservations are no longer so naive. This disenchantment with planning was inevitable. First, the idea was enormously oversold. Early on, formal planning systems gained momentum and steamrollered any criticisms that they couldn't live up to their promise.

Secondly, companies wanted to believe. The experience with planning can be compared to the introduction of computers into the office, which in itself created a feeling of euphoria. Computers, it was felt, somehow would excuse managers from making tough decisions. Their sheer computing power masked their limits in other directions. Eventually, managers learned how to use computers to make better decisions on their own. Similarly, formal plans inflated expectations at first. Given better planning, higher profits were presumed to follow. This connection between planning and profits became suspect in the 1970s and early 1980s, when fluctuations of the business cycle severely tested the assumptions behind the rush to plan. Good plans helped, but they were no panacea. Many companies did no better with planning than they had done before. Planning has real benefits — such as providing a means for communication and coordination among the parts of a company — but it is no substitute for sound business practices and judgment.

Another problem with planning was the vagueness of the concept. Supposing a newly hired planner was asked to install a planning system. What guidelines would he or she follow? New planners tended to imitate existing systems, and most of the "advanced" systems that were created were not much more than embellishments of the traditional budgeting process. Long-range planning was just coming into vogue in the 1950s, which basically meant that companies were taking longer, more comprehensive views of future trends. It was hailed as a "total" system, enabling firms to prepare systematically for the long term.

Eventually, a routine for long-term planning was standardized. An annual planning cycle tended to become the model for planners, with modifications possible to suit individual cases (see the following figure). More and more companies became long range planners, or claimed to have long-range planning systems. Articles on plans, strategy, and planning strategically threatened to cause an information overload. Practitioners, consultants, and academicians coalesced around this novel, but hardly new, dimension of management.

Despite the technical improvements and the attention lavished on long-range planning, the focus throughout continued to be conspicuously narrow. Stripped of all the cosmetic features, the only formal vehicle for planning long range as described in the literature on planning was contained within the conventional annual planning cycle. The cycle, while presumably attuned to long-range planning concerns, conformed to a twelve-month calendar. At the end of the cycle, divisional budgets had to be approved. It was, in fact, a system designed for internal resource allocation and fed

Typical Annual Planning Cycle

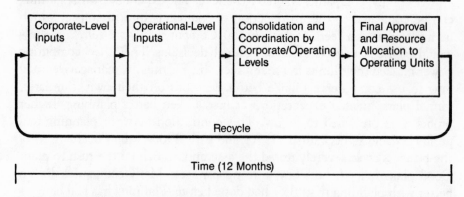

by operational budgets and plans. Designed to serve divisional needs, it was and is ill-suited for corporate-wide restructuring and strategy.

In short, while analysis and planning of current operations was provided for, almost no structural thought was given to planning for change. The term *structural thought* merits emphasizing. There are a number of ad hoc approaches to planning for change. Some companies form committees to address the issues. Others assemble project groups to study specific proposals for restructuring. Still others rely on external advisors, including consultants, investment bankers, directors, or other outsiders. The chief corporate planner may head a number of emergency trouble-shooting teams. Acquisitions and divestments are actively researched by someone, somewhere, in most large companies. Methods, however, are all or mostly all ad hoc approaches to the problem. There is no explicit, ongoing recognition given to dealing with change.

What *has* evolved is the language of planning. "Strategic planning" replaced long-range planning. This attached a greater importance to strategic planning, as opposed to former planning models, but with few specifics to define what strategic planning meant. The word *strategic* became a ubiquitous prefix attached to every aspect of every plan, and many subjects with no connection to planning. Would any planner admit to an unimportant or *non*strategic approach to planning? For this reason, the term *strategic* *planning* is minimized here in order to zero in on the two key elements below that give a more specific and distinguishable character to planning.

1. Where is planning conducted?
2. What type of plan is needed?

WHERE IS PLANNING CONDUCTED?
CORPORATE VS. BUSINESS-LEVEL PLANNING

Planning can be conducted at the corporate level or the business level, depending on whether a firm is growing internally or by external means. Strategy determines where an organization plans. Given a decision to continue a successful past strategy, as in the case of a J. M. Smucker, planning rests with the business units. They have profit responsibility and therefore should develop the supporting strategy and plans. In such cases, the corporate level's involvement is limited. It may coordinate and review the various business plans, but strategy formulation and implementation are left to those who know the competition and the markets and also have the responsibility for producing the desired results.

With corporate-wide restructuring, the shoe is on the other foot. Business managers lack the necessary perspective and objectivity to develop strategy for the entire firm. Only at the top organizational level can decisions be made that cut across businesses. Depending on the situation, there are reasons to raise the efficiency of particular businesses, or the effectiveness of the entirety by changing its mix of businesses. Mesta Machine's corporate "efficiency" could not overcome the drop in demand for its products. Shrinking or declining markets generally offer poor long-term potential regardless of how efficiently a company might manage its affairs. Conversely, even the fastest growing markets are no cure for inept management. Squeezing maximum performance from existing businesses obviously is important, whatever the corporate-level strategy.

As a company evolves, it may need to shift planning gears. In some cases, a successful grand strategy need not be disturbed. A Smucker, or McDonald's, or K mart turn in superior results year after year and remain devoted to a core business. In other companies, this commitment is not shared. More and more corporations are finding reasons to diversify. Conglomerates in particular exemplify an extreme shift away from single-industry dependency. By diversifying, companies no longer need rely exclusively on the sum of their parts. Underperforming units can be sold, raising overall results, and new businesses can be acquired, also with the idea of bettering a firm's performance.

Planning clearly should remain with line managers as long as resources are going back into operations. This commonsense argument becomes a partial view of strategy when resources are being allocated outside the company. An actively evolving company cannot go to business level managers for direction. In this case, the corporate level must assert the primacy of its planning role and develop its own planning mechanism. The more a company seeks to change its current profile, the less applicable is a highly stylized approach oriented to business level planning.

Because the tendency toward unrelated diversification is fairly recent, the planning systems of many companies have failed to differentiate between planning for operations and planning to diversify away from them. For most firms, all planning was supervised by headquarters' professional staff planners. They stepped into their new positions with few preconceptions. Encouraged by a passive chief executive office, and having his or her tacit authority, they attempted to play an active role in developing business-level plans. This interference at the business level was later reversed. Chief executives disenchanted with the results of strategic planning diminished the size of corporate staffs and increased responsibility for strategy and plans by the business level, with little regard to whether strategy suggested a business level initiative.

Muddling around in search of a proper match between plans and strategy has been a fundamental problem with so-called strategic planning. Envisioned as a powerful new engine for profits, and later as a failed experiment, corporate staffs have been the targets of disappointed executives. In corporations, it is traditional to fire the team rather than the coach.

General Motors provides a striking example of the mishandling of corporate strategic planning. Although Chairman Roger B. Smith of GM introduced strategic planning in 1971, he finally gave up on a headquarters' planning initiative after several failed attempts to make it work. Planning is now decentralized and divisional heads carry the responsibility for planning within their own units. This, of course, is how it should have been. At the time, GM was striving to become a more efficient car manufacturer. Given this strategy, GM's divisions could only lose flexibility and initiative at the busines level by having a corporate corps of planners tell them how to plan their operations. Headquarters still controlled finances, and thus the important function of deciding which plans got funded. This left considerable discretionary power for the chief executive's office while leaving divisional strategy and plans to division heads.

Corporate level staff planners should have assisted business-level planners and consolidated the plans of the various divisions for a single overall view of GM's future thrusts. But they could not carry responsibility for plans they did not have the authority to implement. The following figure makes this distinction by separating a corporate coordinating role in planning from a primary corporate role for developing strategy initiatives. As indicated, when the corporate level is engaged in reshaping a company's

Hierarchy of Corporate- and Business-Level Planning

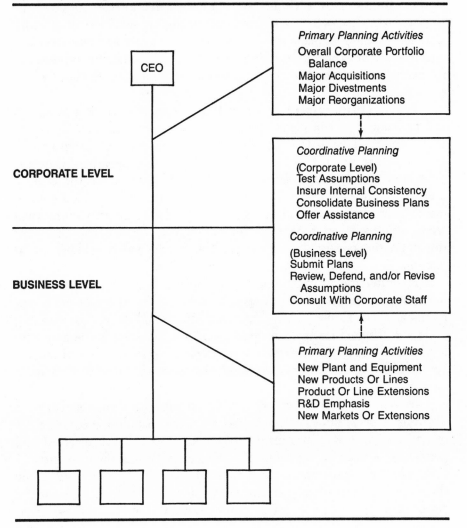

basic structure — through acquisitions, divestments, or major reorganizations — it assumes an identity and function apart from its everyday duties in helping line managers to plan. Consequently, now that GM seems intent on major restructuring, including possible future non-car acquisitions, it cannot afford to rely solely on the planning directions given by its division heads.

Revolution against strategic planning was due in part to confusion regarding the role to be played by corporate-level planners. On one plane, the corporate level is designed into the annual planning cycle. It typically begins the process by providing guidelines and assumptions to be included in the business plans, such as a standard economic forecast, or "critical" corporate-wide issues to be addressed, like energy consumption or inflation. Detailed operational plans are then written. Corporate and business planners iron out any differences of interpretation, and a final plan is presented for executive review. Based on this document, resources are allocated internally.

A coordinating corporate role within the annual plan is a minimum and permanent part of planning in almost any large company. Corporate staff planners serve as facilitators, ensuring a smoothly operating system. But they have no authority to override business planners. In this or any situation where the future of a firm is determined by operations, the leverage is exerted by line management. If it came to a confrontation with divisional management, corporate planners normally would lose. Chief executives will sacrifice staff advisors rather than those directly responsible for profits. This rule of relative power is perhaps responsible for the widely held belief that planning is strictly a line manager's responsibility.

Planning the restructuring of a company, however, is a decidedly different proposition. Neither responsibilities nor results are linked to operational plans. Consequently, business planners and the annual planning cycle are ill-suited for this contingency. Direct planning at the corporate level is implied and a second mechanism in planning for change is necessary. For diversifying firms, this second dimension to planning is even more crucial.

In sum, coordination of business-level planning is a minimum of good planning in most firms. It is necessary merely to handle the complexities of size and diversity. Eventually, this function will be as accepted and permanent as such departmental functions as marketing, finance, production, etc. An equally important but distinct part in planning is played by the corporate level when companies diversify. Only headquarters has the perspective and authority to plan corporate-wide changes. In these cases, formulation of strategy, development of specific plans, and their execution must be controlled directly from the top.

Depending on the circumstances, a company may need to bolster its planning efforts at the corporate or business level. A necessary first condition, however, is to appreciate the difference between the two. To my knowledge, no serious effort has been made to develop a separate corporate-level approach to planning for diversifying companies. Without such a rationale, companies will keep trying to shoehorn their planning activities into a system designed for an earlier period and a simpler strategy.

WHAT TYPE OF PLANNING IS NEEDED? CREATIVE VS. ROUTINE PLANNING

In addition to the proper organizational level, a second factor to consider is whether planning is creative or routine in nature. Creative planning is indicated when significant shifts in strategy and investment occur. A unit reevaluating its basic competitive position within its market is one possibility. Moving into a new market with new competitors is another. Venturing overseas for the first time and in a major way is a third option.

Routine plans are perfectly adequate for firms pursuing a routine strategy. McDonald's, for example, emphasizes a few key elements like cleanliness, customer service, quality ingredients, and consistency. Sticking to these basics, McDonald's has left its competitors behind. Repetition of a successful pattern is one of the secrets of excellence, according to Peters and Waterman in *In Search of Excellence*. Given the right environment, the demands on planning can be modest indeed. In a firm like McDonald's, where the same guiding philosophy prevails, formal plans tend to be repetitious. Once learned, a planning routine will not stimulate a manager to daring new adventures. That does not mean plans are unnecessary or unimportant. It *does* suggest that planning is not the major contributor to profits. The level of results in these cases depends on careful attention to details.

For companies desiring to change, a second creative side to planning is indicated. Companies diversifying away from a single focus on the food business — like Pillsbury, General Mills, or Consolidated Foods — require a more complete approach to planning than McDonald's. For active conglomerates, this second aspect of planning is imperative. Also, in diversified companies, planning can be either creative or routine at the corporate or business levels. The following matrix combines the elements of organiza-

A Matrix of Planning Styles
(By Organizational Level and Degree of Innovativeness)

ORGANIZATIONAL LEVEL

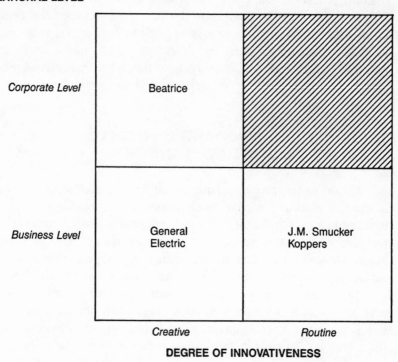

	Creative	Routine
Corporate Level	Beatrice	
Business Level	General Electric	J.M. Smucker Koppers

DEGREE OF INNOVATIVENESS

tional levels and innovativeness to show how the two interact. Four companies are used to illustrate the type of planning represented by this matrix.

General Electric, for example, provides a case of a dynamic but operations-driven company. Because GE's overall strategy depends on excelling in each of its present businesses, the business level carries the burden for planning. Creative planning is indicated because of the internal dynamics of major businesses. Several units are involved in developing a full line of services and equipment for the automated factory of the future. Others are actively evolving to become or remain high-tech leaders. Finally, acquisitions and divestments are part of a strategy to improve competitive positions of others. Some product lines of GE, such as light bulbs and small household appliances, on the other hand, require little innovative strategy. Momentum growth in these mature markets may be all that is expected. Here, routine long range planning will do.

In sum, for a very diversified company like GE, every business is not innovating at the same time or with the same level of intensity. The estimated high degree of innovativeness in many of GE's major business units suggest its placement in the lower left position in the matrix.

This reading of GE's situation would raise disclaimers from some of its managers. Not wishing to be depicted as merely routine, they would argue that their activities are creative. Any definition not spelled out in concrete terms will cause argument. Reactions can be anticipated similar to those of executives when asked to classify themselves as either "leaders" or "managers." When Professor Abraham Zaleznik of Harvard University uses his ploy of dividing participants in his executive seminars into these two categories, individuals invariably see themselves as leaders or combination leader-managers. Few like the less dynamic image of "manager." Terms like *hard-working, methodical,* and *fair-minded* seem pedestrian when compared to *visionary, spontaneous,* and *energetic.* In a like fashion, *routine* suffers in comparison to *creative* when referring to planning.

Despite these semantic difficulties, a distinction between the two types of planning is useful. If nothing else, it makes the point often lost in the literature that plans are not carbon copies to be duplicated from one company to another. There are different types of plans suitable for companies following different strategies. Routine plans and creative plans characterize the range between change and stability, representing rapidly diversifying conglomerates at one extreme and steady-state, single-industry firms at the other.

Beatrice occupies the far end of that spectrum. Although widely diversified, like GE, Beatrice depends on significant corporate-level restructuring to provide for future growth and performance. Its strategy of unrelated diversification requires close supervision by headquarters and a highly creative approach to developing a new family of business groups. These two dimensions ultimately will decide the success of its restructuring strategy. Beatrice's situation puts it in the upper left quadrant, indicating both a corporate level focus and a creative element to planning.

Koppers also is a widely diversified company. Unlike Beatrice or GE, however, Koppers is not innovating. Its management style tends to be conservative and it has remained positioned in large, mature markets. Within such a static state, creative planning plays a relatively minor role in Koppers's ability to outperform its competitors. This task, rather, rests with the ability of its business managers to outexecute their counterparts. Until Koppers articulates dynamic new strategies for its major businesses or the corporation as a whole, incremental planning adjustments should do. This suggests a routine rather than creative approach to planning and one led by its line managers. Fine-tuning the present system until strategy itself changes and suggests innovativeness in planning will keep Koppers on its present course.

Finally, J. M. Smucker's place in the matrix reflects a fundamentally unchanged strategy and therefore limited planning needs. Very successful in its pursuit of a specific niche for itself, Smucker's apparent aim is to continue to dominate the "jam and preserves" segment of the food business. Emphasis rests with the ability of its divisional managers to execute this strategy. Given its long history of competing in this market, planning is more routine than creative, with the necessary apparatus of formal planning relatively simple and mechanistic. Decisions in Smucker's case, as in Kopper's, depend on the emphasizing of the fundamentals and details rather than of imaginative new strategies and risks.

The upper-right-hand box in the matrix is deliberately left empty. Theoretically, a company in that box would conduct routine planning at the corporate level. But this is a contradiction. Companies that plan routinely require only a business-level strategy. Nonroutine planning at the corporate level would shift a company into the upper left box. There are, in sum, only three possibilities: either creative planning at the corporate or business level, or routine business planning.

A swing to unrelated diversification lasting several decades would logically suggest greater numbers of companies moving into the upper left quadrant of the matrix. In actuality, creative planning at the corporate level has been minimal. The scales remain overweighted in favor of business-level plans and strategy. In practice and theory, then, competitive strategy *within existing industry structures* is the prevailing view.

This focus on the business side of planning has been reinforced by Michael Porter's influential book, *Competitive Strategy*. Although more scholarly in tone than most general business books, it was enthusiastically embraced by practitioners. Without detracting in the slightest from the high quality of Porter's text, a large measure of its success is probably attributable to its reinforcement of what companies wanted to hear. Emphasis is on refining and improving the familiar task of competitive strategy. Planners at the business level need strive only for additional sophistication in the traditional methods of planning.

The technology of business planning and strategy undoubtedly gains from the insights in the Porter book, but at the same time the message that comes through is that this is the only level worth planning for. It tends to elevate the "science" of business-level planning above the less scientific but critical aspect of corporate-wide change. In a survey by Booz-Allen &

Hamilton of 3,000 senior managers, 86 percent of whom were dissatisfied with their current planning, "the widespread use of 'sophisticated' planning techniques has often been cited as a key contributor to the decline of innovation."[2]

CREATIVE PLANNING AT THE CORPORATE LEVEL — THE MISSING LINK

In the 1950s and 1960s, when the strategy of unrelated diversification cried out for creative top-level planning, the actual job of planning fell to professional staff technicians. Instead of dynamic leadership, companies turned to cold analysis — a trend that continues today. An insightful comment by the founder of Apple Computer, Stephen P. Jobs, gives a succinct view of the problems of planning in large companies, which of course applies with even more force to large diversified organizations:

"Go back ten years. Polaroid and Xerox would have been on everyone's list of the ten best-managed companies. How did they lose their way when they became multibillion-dollar corporations? When you start growing like that, you start adding middle management like crazy. . . . People in the middle have no understanding of the business, and because of that, they screw up communications. To them, it's just a job. The corporation ends up with mediocre people that form a layer of concrete. We're trying to keep Apple as flat as possible."[3]

In Japan, corporations had no large planning staffs or elaborate planning processes. Japan's position in many of its confrontations with U.S. businesses benefited from the informality of planning. Lack of a specialized staff forced a greater concentration on corporate strategy by the chief executive officer and a flexible rather than a tightly structured view of opportunities. Japan's leaders were forced to sharpen the creative side of planning, based on their leader's instincts rather than technical staff expertise. As the Japanese-born Director of McKinsey & Company's consulting operations in Japan has noted: "Insight is the key to this process. Because it is creative, partly intuitive, and often disruptive of the status quo, the resulting plans might not even hold water from the analyst's point of view. It is the creative element in these plans and the drive and will of the mind that conceived them that give these strategies their extraordinary competitive impact."[4]

Interestingly, the same authority now believes that this informal style of top-level strategy must be superseded by more disciplined corporate planning. The personal initiatives of the past will not be adequate for the complex world of the future. However, the focus on the corporate level will persist. Even as major U.S. corporations strive to push strategic planning ever lower in the organization, "a number of Japanese are moving in the opposite direction. . . . Japanese companies are learning that an overemphasis on planning at the business level unit can be dangerous."[5]

Will American firms be outplanned again? Unless the lessons of the past are better assimilated, the possibility is very real. What has passed for strategic planning in many firms is not much more than a reaction to crises. Disenchanted with strategic planning as orchestrated by corporate staff planners, companies have given all planning responsibility to business managers instead. This sacrifices the corporate role in planning instead of facing up to it.

Executives of diversifying companies that rely either on staff-driven corporate planning or business-level planners are foresaking their duties as their companys' chief strategists. They are relying on approaches that lack creativeness or a proper perspective. Business-level planners cannot exert authority over any higher organizational level. Also, their views are narrowed by self-interest. These conditions create the circumstance for a separate corporate-level role, as illustrated in the following chart. A corporate planning function is indicated apart from merely coordination of and assistance with operating units' plans. In addition, three tips for this "primary" planning role are: keep the staff small, make the system flexible, and don't build it to last forever.

What Kind of Top Planner Do You Need?

Experts insist that a company's chief planner is always its chief executive officer. This is true in the sense of a final authority. Yet the reality is that heads of major divisions of many large and diversified companies are assuming responsibilities comparable to CEOs. Sector executives in General Electric, for example, consolidate and rationalize the plans of groups, divisions and departments. In other companies, group executives play similar roles as do sector executives in General Electric. At Bristol Myers, three presidents were named to head each of the company's main divisions. According to the firm's chairman and CEO, each president would function

Keeping the Corporate and Business Planning Staffs Separate

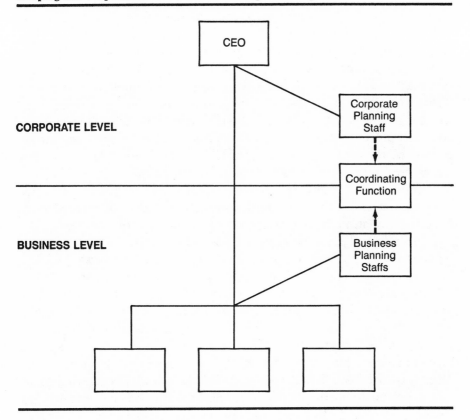

as chief operating officer of his own group with "full responsibility for its strategic, operational and organizational leadership."

The point is that increasing size and complexity in American industry is pushing important planning responsibilities to lower levels in the organization. In General Electric, for instance, each of five sector executives would be responsible for running a $6 billion business, assuming General Electric's 1984 sales of nearly $30 billion were equally divided among its five sectors. Each group executive is similarly responsible for supervising operations that generate hundreds of millions in annual revenues. This means General Electric's sector executives are responsible for operations that are larger than half of the industrial companies listed in the *Fortune 500*, and its group executives for operations easily among the top *Fortune 1000* largest industrial firms.

New Strategists for New Strategies

Until the middle of this century, companies operated within a particular industry so that business- and corporate-level perspectives coincided. Also, CEOs generally were trained and experienced in the business so that they could act effectively as their own best strategist. Strategy in such instances often demanded creativity, but not in the same meaning as modern-day restructuring or repositioning of a company into unrelated businesses. During that time, guiding a company through the growing pains of greater size and related diversification was an enormously creative challenge. Correspondingly, the creativity and skills of CEOs influenced which companies ultimately prospered and which ones faltered or failed.

Then as now, thinking creatively meant thinking differently. Henry Ford was one such thinker. He detested the formality of management. Instead of imitating the practice of buying suppliers, as other car manufacturers had done, Ford went a step further and built his own parts. He also supplied the huge River Rouge works in Dearborn with its own coal and iron ore reserves, and built a steel-making plant nearby. His grand vision was to build a completely integrated operation from raw materials to finished products. Details were often left to others, including day-to-day operations.

Ford barely disguised his disdain for the "organizational genius" of Alfred Sloan of General Motors. Ford's instincts for leadership clashed with Sloan's penchant for organized management. Where Ford was instinctive, Sloan was analytical. Where Ford made bold breakthroughs allowing quantum jumps on competitive advantage, Sloan developed the structure and strategy that would carry GM into the multibillion-dollar era of modern automakers. In the end, Sloan's organizational skills and long-term strategy proved more enduring than Ford's entrepreneurial successes. Throughout business history it has been demonstrated that organizational demands of size and complexity will eventually put brakes on the progress of sheer personal genius.

Ford was a brilliant creator and builder of his epoch. Sloan anticipated the needs of the future. Neither top executive benefited from formal planning as it is known today. At the time, planning was in an embryonic stage, and strategy, such as it was, depended on the personal qualities of those who led their organizations. In this context, both Ford and Sloan were creative thinkers, although they differed dramatically in style.

In a modern setting, Ford would be typical of the entrepreneurial managers who engineered the first conglomerates. Alfred Sloan resembles more closely the latter-day diversifiers, like the CEOs of a Coke or Sears who anticipate and plan systematically for change. In the first case, the reliance on formal planning would be minimal. Sloan, with his bent for organizational logic, would take a more measured and analytical approach to planning corporate-wide restructuring. An interesting speculation is what kind of organizational structures Sloan would have built to deal with each contingency.

The lessons of history suggest the importance of the structural side of diversification. In time, companies must learn to manage what has been acquired. Conglomerates like LTV, ITT, Whittaker, U.S. Industries, Colt Industries, Greyhound, Fuqua Industries, and Brunswick are struggling to find such organizational solutions. The genius of Alfred Sloan would be welcome. Without this unlikely reincarnation, the emphasis should switch at least to the disciplined but creative side of organization. Sprawling empires must put their houses in order for lasting operational synergy. This means a focus at the corporate level that views creatively the task of rationalizing acquired businesses into a unified organization.

ACQUISITIONS PLANNING

An important and novel responsibility for the corporate level in diversifying firms is planning how different businesses will fit together. Because acquisitions are the main avenue for adding businesses, a first strategy to be mastered is the art of planning acquisitions. Rationalizing these acquired businesses into logical business groupings is an important second phase. Both aspects require different talents. Planning which companies to buy, for instance, demands more creativity than is commonly supposed. A conventional early practice was to define very specific criteria for an acquisition — then try to find companies that fit the ideal. This approach is increasingly out of touch with a changing marketplace. As more and more companies have diversified, there are fewer undiversified or "ideal" firms to acquire. This means that acquirors often are forced to buy considerably more assets than they need in order to get the pieces they want.

Despite the long odds, systematic searches for ideal acquisitions continues to be the model for many companies. Criteria are carefully established, a list of acquisition candidates is developed, and then a search for companies to suit the predetermined guidelines ensues. This common pattern has been described in the literature on diversification and followed in many companies' diversification programs. It is an approach that lends itself to a tightly structured analysis, including the use of sophisticated screening techniques and financial evaluations to identify potential candidates for purchases. It reasonably assumes that the proper identification of an acquisition is a major element in a successful diversification.

Yet this process of identification, as currently envisioned, has time and again been frustrated by the realities of an imperfect market for acquisitions: what is desirable is often not available and what can be purchased may not fit the overall plan. Because the market will become less and less "perfect" as more and more companies continue to diversify, firms must adopt a diversification strategy to suit these circumstances. This means a less rigid approach to formulating precise guidelines for diversification and a more pragmatic approach to dealing with available acquisition opportunities.

For instance, ConAgra, a diversified food company, has made a number of acquisitions but not in the businesses it would have predicted or chosen. Banquet Foods, one of its success stories, became available as a result of RCA's divestiture program. Peavey, a grain and flour milling company, was bought at a distress price when the profits in that industry were at a nadir. A more recent acquisition, Armour Food, was purchased from the Greyhound Corporation, conditioned on a lower cost structure for employees. All of these acquisitions required a flexible attitude rather than accurate forecasts of available candidate companies. None of the firms exactly fit ConAgra's previously expressed interest in acquiring commodity businesses, such as poultry. But as the chief executive officer of ConAgra put it, the company has learned to take "a pragmatic, opportunistic approach to expansion: any food-related company with significant market shares, good management, and low product costs is a potential acquisition target."

This example does not diminish the value of having a plan in mind. It merely switches emphasis from targeting for specific firms that fit exacting criteria to developing broader parameters consistent with a company's mission and its distinctive competences. Rather than forecasting results, planners would define areas of compatibility and remain flexible on specific opportunities that might arise to fulfill its needs. Perhaps Peter Drucker had this aspect in mind when he suggested that companies must plan because they cannot accurately forecast.

Planning how to integrate acquisitions, on the other hand, is more amenable to a formal routine. It is in this phase that businesses are rationalized and strategic groups formed. These types of actions benefit from traditional tools of planning, such as the portfolio matrix, the experience curve, and application of PIMSs findings. Once a company is acquired, planning staffs can do a thorough evaluation, with business-level analysis determining the strategy for obtaining maximum synergy. After ConAgra acquired Banquet Food, for instance, the acquisition was quickly turned around by following a formula comprised of cost-reduction, quality improvements, and new product introductions. A similar approach is indicated for ConAgra's acquisition of Armour Food.

Controlling the Pace and Timing of Acquisitions

John R. Beckett guided Transamerica into many a new business. As its head, he supervised a company engaged in insurance, manufacturing, film distribution, car rental, and air transportation. Yet even Beckett was alarmed by acquisitions programs that pyramided company upon company and borrowing upon borrowing. Unrelated diversification entails risks. Growing faster than acquisitions can be digested is a major one. Appraising the scene in the mid-1960s, Beckett said:

> There are a number of things that distinguish nonsensical pyramiding from a well-run acquisition program. First of all, there are only so many companies that you can buy in a year; to make intelligent decisions you've got to have a great deal of information. You've got to study the alternatives to getting into that section of the economy . . . Secondly, after you make the acquisitions, unless you can run the company as well or better than it was run before, then you don't get a contribution. Usually, it takes two or three years to integrate it into your way of control, your way of doing things, your way of planning. Until then, it doesn't feel comfortable."[6]

Beckett's advice is as good today as when first given. Conglomerate-style diversification needs to be taken at a sustainable pace. As the following chart shows, the maximum synergy of unrelated diversification comes from *combining* different businesses with managerial control of those businesses. Whatever disrupts managerial efficiency upsets this balance. When a company is actively diversifying, for example, it is at the expense of managerial efficiency, since changing structures can't be tightly controlled. Companies acquiring and divesting businesses don't generally give equal leadership and motivation to running operations. It is a simple matter of priorities and management skills. Top managers good at one task are seldom as good at the other. And even if this were not so, major repositioning tends to take a preoccupying part of top management's attention.

Companies typically go through a number of diversification cycles in order to achieve the desired plateau of diversification, as has been noted.

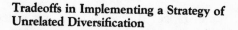

Tradeoffs in Implementing a Strategy of Unrelated Diversification

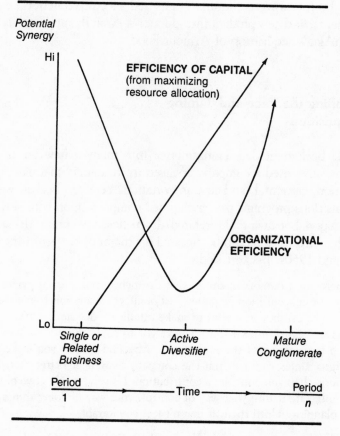

With a few exceptions like General Electric and Minnesota Mining and Manufacturing, companies have not been diversifying long enough to have reached that stage and also to have integrated their various businesses. That means the majority of diversifiers will be alternatively active in either extending their span of businesses or imposing administrative systems. Until a desired equilibrium is approached, the necessary diversification moves will continue to defeat the managerial objective — a kind of Catch – 22 that requires a delicate balance between moving too quickly and failing to move.

Textron provides a good example of the unexpected scenarios that a company might encounter before becoming a mature conglomerate. Textron began inauspiciously enough as a small textile operation called American Woolen. Perceiving a dismal long-term outlook for textiles, Royal Little, the founder of Textron, switched into other businesses, hiring Rupert Thompson to help him manage the diversification program. Textron pushed into a great many unrelated products, including helicopters, watchbands, staplers, lawn mowers, chain saws, and more. The company was, as Royal Little readily admitted, a pure conglomerate striving for a higher return on capital through product diversification.

The hectic pace of Textron's diversification cycles in the first two decades or so have slackened noticeably during the last ten years. The company switched to refocusing its energies inward, toward improving the way it managed its wide array of existing businesses. This natural change of pace — a transitional phase oriented to administration of diversity — broke off abruptly in late 1984 when Textron proposed to acquire Avco, itself a conglomerate, though somewhat less diversified than Textron.

A nominal economic reason for the Avco acquisition was the addition of new businesses, like insurance, and the fit with shared businesses in aerospace. More bluntly, it appeared as a defense against unfriendly takeovers, since Avco was a complex and debt-laden company to digest. Having recently beaten back a proposal to be acquired by a company much smaller than itself, Textron's executives apparently wished to provide themselves with insurance against another takeover attempt.

Acquiring Avco is not what outsiders or even Textron could have predicted. But such uncertainties are commonplace in conglomerate history. Carefully detailed blueprints for success in diversification don't exist. Few companies design the exact contours of their acquisitions programs. The successful ones are those quickest to seize opportunity and adapt to change. In Textron's case, what it may hope to gain are some product and financial synergies. What it gives up is managerial efficiency — and time. In effect, it took a step sideways in its evolution to a mature conglomerate, a detour that diverts top management's attention from administration to reorganization. Avco's operations must be regrouped with Textron's own, and a new managerial structure put into place to supervise the new business groupings. Only then can Textron renew its efforts toward integration of all its "groups" into an effectively operating single organization.

Companies in the best position to pursue a controlled and selective program of unrelated diversification are those already skilled in managing diversified — but not conglomerate — organizations, such as Procter & Gamble, Anheuser-Busch, and Citicorp. They already have large core businesses that can give stability to their diversification program. In addition, they have strong and cohesive cultures that can assimilate major acquisitions as part of a measured and systematic diversification program. Companies like Coke, Sears, and American Express have begun their multi-group diversification strategies, and they have solid core businesses as well as bases of distinctive competences on which to build. Companies lacking their advantages must overcome giant administrative hurdles before making it.

In sum, making acquisitions doesn't follow a linear path of events. Although the process is often envisioned as a sequential one of establishing goals, surveying the population of existing firms and selecting optimum choices, the real world seldom is so accommodating. Companies generally are faced with greater uncertainties than this purely rational method would suggest.

Also, difficulties will arise if corporate staffs decide to lead the post-acquisition program rather than assist. A good rule to keep in mind is: When in doubt, let the business level do business-level planning. In a few cases, this may not be immediately possible, as when an acquisition is one part of a completely new business unit. But as soon as practical, let the business unit assume responsibility for the business plan. Only when profit and planning responsibility reside in the same unit can major operational synergies make significant headway.

Over time, as companies develop a sense of the strategy of making acquisitions, it should be apparent that a successful acquisition plan is in fact a two-part process requiring a natural division of talents. In the formulation stage, a broad corporate-level perspective is needed, with an emphasis on establishing parameters consistent with a company's areas of expertise, and an idea of what type of company it is striving to become. This in turn elevates the concept of mission — what a company is to become — to an importance beyond that generally accorded.

Commonly, a company's perception of its mission is acknowledged as valuable, but only in a brief prelude before proceeding to detail the particulars of formal planning. This attention to getting things done rather than doing the right things is symptomatic of an overload of planning ideas and knowledge that emphasize business-level planning. Prior to the mid-1950s, when corporate growth relied on reinvestment within an industry and diversification was internally generated, this emphasis was deserved. With the phenomenon of unrelated acquisitions and conglomerate-style strategy, however, such a preoccupation is inconsistent with overall performance. Pre-acquisition planning and post-acquisition rationalization are equally important. But they pose different problems. The most successful companies will be those that separate the less formal process of formulating a diversification mission with the more exacting task of implementation.

Notes

1. John D. C. Roach, "From Strategic Planning to Strategic Performance: Closing the Achievement Gap," *Outlook,* Spring 1981, p. 19.
2. Ibid., p. 24.
3. *Business Week,* November 26, 1984, p. 156.
4. *The Mind of the Strategist,* p. 2.
5. *Business Week,* October 1, 1984, p. 71.
6. *Forbes,* September 15, 1967, p. 312.

8 KNOW THE BUSINESS

ROBOTICS is a booming business. Sales of $2 billion by 1990 have been predicted. Buying the number-one robot maker would be an acquisition coup. Right? Westinghouse's experience says otherwise. In 1983, Westinghouse bought the top U.S. robot maker, Unimation. In 1984, it found that Unimation's biggest customers — American automakers — were switching to other types of robots. With the switch went much of the rationale for the acquisition. Not only were customers like Chrysler using different models, they were considering replacement of the Unimates they had already installed.

What went wrong? Just about everything. For starters, Unimation's products were practically obsolete when the company was purchased. Their hydraulic systems leaked oil, which was troublesome when assembling or painting new cars. Besides, repairs required separate hydraulics and electronics workmen. By contrast, electric motor drives are more accurate, don't leak, and only require one repairman. Since electrical equipment is Westinghouse's stock in trade, one wouldn't think that would be their stumbling block. According to one account, it was an avoidable disaster: "There wasn't a whole lot of understanding of what they were getting into."

Hindsight improves everyone's vision, of course. The point is not to single out Westinghouse for special censure. At a cost of $107 million, it wasn't — in financial terms at least — that costly a mistake. Westinghouse's experience is symptomatic of a much wider problem. In the rush to diversify, companies have placed much greater emphasis on the financial and legal aspects of acquisitions than understanding the business. A suspect policy under any conditions, this is particularly risky when diversifying into unrelated businesses.

The essence of making successful acquisitions hinges on two separate elements. As discussed earlier, the acquiror should have a distinctive competence. But equally important is how well that competence fits in with the new business. On the latter point, an understanding of the target business is fundamental. Yet this base of understanding is rarely fully developed before the move, if indeed it is even part of the acquisition process.

Every business has certain "keys" that are essential to its success. Identifying them is not always easy. But it is amazing how few companies even try. Even insiders can be naive about what makes their business tick. Ask executives what the key factors are in their field and you get such generic answers as profit margins, market share, or return on investment. These things are important to *any* successful strategy, but fail to differentiate one business from the next. Keys to success were just as important in the past. New methods of freezing and preserving meats unlocked the way for Swift, Armour, and Cudahy to become national meat packers. They had to develop the network of refrigerated railroad cars and cold storage facilities in addition to overcoming the resistance of consumers to eating meat killed several days or weeks earlier. But refrigeration was the key without which the other considerations would not even have been raised.

General Electric also faced an early dilemma peculiar to its electrical equipment business. Unlike other mass producers, GE could not take advantage of economies of scale without first assisting in the building of a market for its products. Thus it became heavily involved in financing its utility customers to help create a system of power-generating stations and ancillary facilities that would buy its electrical products.

Today's keys to success differ from those in the past. As industries matured, companies accommodated their size and range of activities to the economies of the business. If this meant vertical integration, as in the case of the meat packers, it has long since been achieved and therefore ceases to be a current key factor for success. What is important now is to discover how major businesses have been shaped by time, circumstances, and competition.

What are today's keys? In a few cases, the answers are obvious. Industries typified by high fixed costs and specialized equipment like shipbuilding, steel-making, and oil drilling platforms still benefit from economies of scale. Without a high utilization of the sunk costs in plant and equipment, firms in these industries cannot generate the economies they were designed for. Key factors once identified often seem apparent enough. In reality, uncovering one or two keys within a complex setting of inter-acting factors is exceedingly difficult. Knowing every detail of every stage of operation is clearly not possible or necessary. One or two critical aspects is usually all that is required. Appreciating the value of industry keys before making an acquisition, and pursuing the investigation with determination, are basic hurdles that can be negotiated and that contribute to a more successful acquisition strategy.

ANALYTICAL APPROACHES TO FINDING THE KEYS TO SUCCESS

Two ways exist to find out how industries work. One is to understand the industry itself in some detail, and the other is to study the participants within an industry. The latter course attempts to identify winning and losing strategies and imitate the former. This approach relies on a com-petitive strategy approach: studying your competitors in order to outcompete them. But this approach by itself has drawbacks. It focuses on what com-petitors do, but doesn't always reveal why they do it or whether it is the best thing for someone else to do. Secondly, it veils changes that might be currently underway. By concentrating on the present, future shifts in em-phasis are masked and often overlooked.

Outthinking the competition is a more subtle — and often more successful — maneuver than outmuscling it. By systematically tearing a business down and revealing key relationships, strategy can be tailored and focused. Also in studying why strategy works, a company can anticipate moves before it is forced to change. No single method applies in every circumstance. An industry "breakdown" is a painstaking undertaking and one or more approaches as suggested below may be appropriate.

Value Added

The structure of an industry can be characterized by the value added at each stage of production. For analysis, the difference between costs of materials and sales price are illustrated in the following chart for a hypo-thetical specialty paper products manufacturer. Where the difference be-tween costs and price — or value added — is low, so is the potential for profits. Even with above-average efficiency, a thin margin restricts rewards. From the chart, we can see that conversion of the raw materials into

'Value Added' Stages for a Hypothetical Specialty Paper Products Company

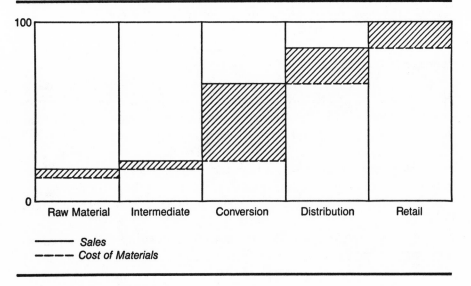

specialty items provides the maximum spread. At this stage, a wide margin exists between price and purchased costs. This does not necessarily mean high profit at this juncture, since competition may also be fierce. But it affords a justification for entry by a company with a special competence in that type of conversion technology. That would be marrying competence with potential, which is all a company can hope for. Companies like Emerson Electric and White Consolidated, which are known for very tight cost controls and efficient operations, might use value added in leveraging this type of competence into businesses with a high value added component and outdated production techniques or lax controls over costs.

Functional Activities

In addition to value added, the functional activities at each stage of production may themselves be keys to a product's sale. Which activity in the chain from sourcing of raw materials to the end product is the most critical? Philip Morris's acquisition of Seven-Up demonstrated the key role of a bottling network for newcomers to the soft drink business. Similarly, distribution is a key function for the beer industry. With its vast network of beer wholesalers, G. Heileman can not only efficiently market its many different labels of beer with its strategy of different brands for different regions, it can also use this wholesaler strength to push additional products through the pipeline, illustrated by its entry into the popular new wine product called California Cooler.

The following table illustrates the key functions associated with a few major industries. For example, in mining heavy and inexpensive raw materials, like aggregates for road building or clay for making bricks, transportation is a limiting factor. Because of the relative abundance and cheapness of aggregate and clay, transportation becomes a high portion of the delivered price. With transport costs escalating rapidly with distance, the economies of these businesses suggest markets close to where the product is mined. Clearly, it is neither a high-tech business nor one susceptible to sophisticated management techniques. An abundant supply of nearby raw materials, however, can provide a competitive edge for a building supply business.

Each function in the table represents a relationship that has proven important for major industries at certain times. The superior strategist is one who takes a completely fresh perspective to determine how his or her company's competence best fits within the structure of specific industries or, even more important, whether the conventional wisdom still holds. In one case, an entrepreneur who sized up the fertilizer business noticed that raw materials were processed close to their source to gain economies of scale, and then shipped to customers. Why couldn't the processing be done closer to where major customers were located, with quicker deliveries and better service compensating for slightly higher costs? Acting on this insight,

Chain of Key Functional Activities and Illustrative Applications

Key Function	Selected Industries
Raw Materials Supply	High-quality, expensive minerals: uranium, molybdenum.
Transportation Costs	Low-quality, inexpensive raw materials: aggregate, clay, salt.
Integrated Production (Economies of Scale)	Steel, shipbuilding, auto manufacturing.
Distribution Network	Beer, soft drinks.
Marketing	Airlines
Advertising, Promotion	Undifferentiated products and luxuries: aspirins, perfumes.
Servicing	Leasing services: copiers, computers, video products.

he bought and reassembled existing fertilizer plants, where prices were depressed due to low demand, and successfully reengineered the way this business had always been done.

Economies of scale, the most ingrained of all assumptions of efficiency, are being regarded anew in other industries as well. Mini-steel mills and on-site industrial gas facilities contradict the notion that big is always better. By building miniature industrial and medical gas facilities next to the users' plants, or by avoiding the inflexibility of large integrated steel plants, customers' needs can be better served. The customer in the end should always determine the economies of a business. Yet this principle has been lost sight of in many businesses that strove to drive costs ever lower by continuously enlarging the size (and as a consequence reducing the flexibility) of operations.

Customers' "Felt" Needs

Sometimes key aspects are not physical but emotional. Customers may relate to a product or company because of an acquired reputation or image. Aspirins, for example, are scientifically indistinguishable in their effect whether a generic label or a brand name is on the bottle. Yet Bayer aspirin consistently outsells its competitors. If asked to name a chocolate, soft drink, fast food, or computer company, one company and one name would come to most people's minds. Such reputations are impossible to attack by coming at them with a low-cost strategy. They are firmly perceived as being worth more. And if it sells, perception is reality.

Here the strategy of an opponent must take the long view. Sony did not win its reputation for quality overnight, nor did Honda and Toyota preempt their America counterparts at first. Once established, a favorable image is a powerful sales tool. More important for new strategy is whether this advantage can be put to more effective use. Only recently has the consumer recognition for Coke and Sears, and in a more modest way, Hershey, been used offensively in a strategy of diversification. Capitalizing on consumer awareness and trust is still an underutilized part of diversification strategy, but a potent one if properly engineered. Assuming a continuing trend to unrelated diversification, it is only a matter of time before brand awareness gets its own recognition as a weapon of strategy.

Some industries are more difficult to dismantle than others. There is no simple approach to uncovering keys to success. It is a painstaking process of discovery and elimination. Even imperfect knowledge, however, is better than driving by automatic pilot. As Philip Morris's experience with Seven-

Up demonstrated, success in one field cannot simply be imitated for success in another. Each business is unique and each merits objective analysis before committing a company's resources.

PRACTICAL APPROACHES TO FINDING THE KEYS TO SUCCESS

A simple but effective alternative to a purely analytical approach is to ask people questions. Few companies' secrets are buried so deep that they cannot be uncovered with a little legwork. This approach also has the not unconsiderable bonus of forcing involvement by top managers — if it is done properly. An apt comparison is with venture capitalists, who risk their own money on their investments in new companies. Consequently their scrutiny of these businesses is intense and hands-on. They get to know top management intimately. They talk to suppliers, customers, ex-employees, secretaries — anyone who can shed light on what might be avoidable problems.

No one can turn a business inside out and know its every detail except from long experience. If one could, the management of unrelated acquisitions would never be a challenge. The purpose is not to become operationally expert, but merely prudently aware of the risks. For instance, a firm's "hidden problems" are generally known by someone who is willing to talk about them, if the investigation is sufficiently intense. A logical but often neglected source is a company's own line managers.

In many corporations, however, this task of investigation is shunted off to others. There is a tendency to rely on the advice of outside experts. When not closely supervised, these experts substitute their experiences and point of view for that of the client. Used judiciously, consultants are an efficient use of resources. They can also be used as a means of escaping responsibility for decisions, providing management with an "out" when discrepancies are later discovered. This reluctance to be personally involved in the operational details of acquisitions has caused more than a few headaches.

When Exxon purchased Reliance Electric it engaged the top consulting firms of Booz, Allen & Hamilton and Arthur D. Little plus the prestigious banking firm of Morgan Stanley. Yet none of these expert advisors apparently concentrated on the critical feature of the Reliance acquisition — the ability to inexpensively mass-produce a secret device for raising the efficiency of most electric motors. According to reports, neither Exxon nor its advisors questioned the assumption that such energy-efficient motors could be made for drastically less cost, "eventually as much as 90 percent

lower." Once the proposal was examined in detail after Reliance was purchased, the cost estimates were almost immediately discredited.

Exxon's is not an isolated experience. Companies characteristically
emphasize the financial aspects of a deal. Only infrequently do they devote
equal time to studying what it is they are buying. Exxon's senior vice-
president in charge of negotiations in the Reliance deal "prepared himself
by reading an electrical engineering text 'in between television shows.' "
This suggests two comments on the contrast between the approach of
venture capitalists and a large corporation in making investments in companies. First, venture capitalists are likely to be more careful with their
own money at stake, and consequently they are more willing to become
directly involved in the messy details. In Exxon's case, it could have developed an internal production team to evaluate the product before closing
the deal, or insisted on such investigation from the consultants who were
supposed to evaluate its feasibility, or at least covered themselves contrac-
tually to prevent the type of mishap that occurred.

This type of arm's-length analysis is found in new product development as well. In the opinion of the Matsushita Electric Industrial Company,
U. S. manufacturers rely too much on outsiders. They hire others to do
their marketing studies and consumer surveys. At Matsushita, employees
regularly talk to store owners and make house calls to customers to find out
in detail what problems they have with Matsushita products.

Large corporations can gain much from an entrepreneurial approach
to acquisitions. Like good detective work, the evidence builds piece by
piece. It is not glamorous work, but it is necessary. A first step is for managers
to get out of the office. While working on several acquisition proposals
with major corporations, I don't remember one instance when the really
important judgments relied on knowledge of the business or working with
primary sources. The principal tools of analysis were a hand-held calculator
and a team of external experts, the number depending on the size and
importance of the acquisition.

The really successful companies will work more intelligently in making
acquisitions. They will use all the means at their disposal. This includes
more effective use of their own personnel and closer attention to the nitty
gritty details of the environment in which the targeted acquisition operates.
As commonsense as such advice sounds, experience shows it will fall on
deaf ears in most companies. To give another illustration, a video products
division of one of the biggest U. S. corporations began what for it was a
new technique in marketing: its design engineers began communicating
with customers. The idea, it seems, was to get engineers "oriented toward

bringing the technology and the consumer demand together." That this most elementary of all marketing presumptions should be considered "new" must be comforting news to a company like Matsushita. It has been doing that all along and appears more committed, as a matter of basic policy, than companies just beginning to experiment with this novel approach to marketing research.

The major drawback to making secondary research the primary approach is an emphasis on what is readily researchable — but not what is necessarily most critical. Results show what is important and measurable in the consultant's eyes, but this cannot make up for a lack of a personal strategy by management. Only by being personally familiar with a situation can a senior manager get a feel for its potential. This is particularly true in fields that are rapidly changing or deregulating.

In the 1960s, third-party computer leasing was in its infancy. A lot of computer leasing companies sprouted but none were household names, and the concept of buying computers from manufacturers and then leasing them to customers was an unproven idea. Given an assignment to establish the economies of this business for a consulting client, I decided the best place to start was to talk to people in the trade. I gathered a lot of facts — and folklore — about this business that I hadn't appreciated.

For one thing, three keys emerged about the business from my investigation. The ultimate profitability of leases, based on the accounting assumptions used for reporting earnings, depended on estimates of useful lives of equipment and salvage value. In addition, the first two keys depended on a third: the policies of IBM, which in effect set the economic terms for computer equipment under which all third-party lessors were operating. Using liberal or conservative assumptions on salvage value and useful lives permitted leasing companies to vary their levels of earnings. Perhaps most important for an aggressively minded company, however, was the realization that once the desired number of leases had been written, this business generated a large amount of cash for which there was no immediate outlet. In effect, independent leasing companies were cash cows.

One of the biggest of the independent leasing companies — Leasco — anticipated the lessons of the Boston Consulting Group's portfolio matrix and used the cash throw-off from computer leasing to get into a variety of other businesses. Saul Steinberg, the CEO of Leasco, parlayed a modest beginning into ownership of a number of other businesses, leading eventually to ownership of Reliance Group Holdings, one of the fifty largest diversified financial companies in the United States. Saul Steinberg's methods may be unorthodox and even objectionable, but he knew the leasing business and how to use it to amass a much bigger and more diversified organization. The window of opportunity for these third-party computer lessors was wide open for only a short period of time. Those who understood the nature of the business and were willing to take the risks survived the inevitable fallout when latecomers crowded in.

The moral of this story is that it is not enough to see the keys to success; one must act decisively and often early in order to reap handsome profits. An important corollary lesson was that the inflated reported profits from computer leasing was the principal reason that many of these companies were acquired. Only after purchase were the profits found to be ephemeral. Acquirors were attracted to the glitter of the industry without bothering to understand its basics.

COMMON MISTAKES TO AVOID

The corporate landscape is littered with bad acquisitions. Analysis of these disasters could be fruitful in demonstrating what *doesn't* work. That's easier to show than what *does*. In trying to reduce the margin for major errors, a few repeatable mistakes are worth noting. Among the most glaring miscues are the three below.

Number Crunching

Financial projections from combining earnings resulting from an acquisition remains a preoccupying part of acquisition analysis. This short-term focus was especially noticeable in the 1950s and 1960s, when deals were made almost without regard to what companies produced or how they operated. In a typical example, the CEO of Emery Air Freight recalled that when his company was selling at fifty and sixty times earnings, the president of U. S. Industries, a mushrooming conglomerate, said to him: "John, I've got to do something to get my PE multiple up so I can issue more stock and acquire more companies. Let's change our company names to Emery – U.S. Industries so I can borrow some of your mystique to dazzle the stock market."

The worst of such excesses is past, but the inclination for making "financially justified" acquisitions lingers on. Only the code words are different. Discounted cash flow (DCF) replaced price-earnings (PE) multiples. DCF, a popular finance tool, works something like this: An acquisition price is determined by estimating cash flows arising from the acquisition over the next five to ten years, and then calculating the current value of these monies by using a discount rate reflective of risks and the opportunity costs of investment. By using an acceptable rate of return, say 15 percent, the acquiror can tell whether the present value of future cash to be generated by the acquiree exceeds a minimum return on its investment. This basic finance concept has some imaginative variations — like borrowing against an acquiree's assets to fund other businesses — but DCF is at the heart of the financial analysis.

Financial projections are important, of course, but they distort acquisition evaluations when they crowd out other considerations. When a company buys into a business it hasn't first investigated, and then doesn't try to integrate it after the acquisition, it is compounding the chances for major problems. These type of arm's-length acquisitions work out only as long as the business itself continues to fulfill the projections on which it was based. Since the assumptions behind the projections are often tentative, it seldom is a long term formula for success.

In Exxon's purchase of Reliance, for instance, a major part of the evaluation was financial, with Morgan Stanley projecting an annual earnings growth of 1 percent from the acquisition. The present value of this increase in earnings was "somewhat mysteriously calculated to be $610 million, which roughly coincided with the total value of the premium Exxon proposed to offer." What proved to be a crucial blind side to this evaluation — the assumed cost savings of mass production — "was not investigated closely." In the end, Exxon's $600 million premium turned out to be a costly mistake. Exxon's experience is a microcosm of similar types of surprises where acquirors devote more time to developing the numbers than investigating the underlying assumptions.

Hasty or Emotional Commitment

The surface appeal of a transaction shouldn't cause a company to abandon a calculated evaluation based on merits. The old saying, "Invest in haste, repent in leisure" is too often true. First-time mistakes are common among novice diversifiers. Even seasoned acquirors can be beguiled by the appearance of fit into a premature analysis or an overinflated premium. Admittedly, preacquisition investigations may not uncover things that are deliberately swept under the rug. Yet ironically enough, large and experienced companies, expert in their own fields and sophisticated in managing their own businesses, fall victim to the simplest of mistakes when making acquisitions.

Only after Kodak acquired Atex, the dominant supplier of text-editing systems for major magazines and newspapers, did it discover financial and managerial disarray. What seemed from the outside to be an ideal match — offering Kodak entry into markets where it already sold chemicals, film, and other printing supplies — turned into an embarrassment. Key managers began an exodus from a top management team that was weak to begin with. New products were not being developed quickly enough, and the existing product line was aging. Finally, finances needed shoring up. Atex has not been mentioned in Kodak's annual report since its acquisition in 1981, a sign of Kodak's disillusionment with its investment. Kodak needs a stronger commitment than it has shown so far in order to turn Atex around. According to one expert observer, time is running out: "If they don't get it right this time, there won't be anything left."

While the fullest extent of Atex's problems could only be discerned from the inside, normal investigative precautions could have alerted Kodak that real problems existed. It is remarkable that companies not known to be risk-takers, that are indeed meticulously cautious when it comes to internal management, would take a cavalier approach to businesses they are about to enter. How can one explain the abandon with which companies enter unrelated fields with neither serious study nor a distinctive competence? Ashland Oil, for example, sold most of its oil reserves, and severed the ties to the business it knows best, and used the proceeds to buy into an odd-lot assortment of businesses it knew nothing about, including insurance and pollution equipment. A former consultant to the company commented snidely that Ashland's apparent strategy was one of "remaining in a series of unattractive businesses."

No Distinctive Competence

Distinctive competence is a key to unrelated diversification. It doesn't restrict firms to the same business or even related businesses, but it does suggest that knowledge of some facet of a business — whether marketing, distribution, production, or whatever — makes entry feasible, indeed, desirable. This eminently sensible observation is inexplicably violated in case after case. Ashland Oil had no reason to expect it could operate insurance or pollution-control businesses better than those already in those fields, nor that these would be the types of businesses that could run themselves.

Mattel had similarly taken a "random walk" approach to acquisitions. It bought and sold a circus, made investments in pet supplies, movie production, and children's books. It also acquired an ice show. What distinctive competence did Mattel see in such a group of businesses, or in any one of them, for that matter? One possible explanation is that in diversifying, Mattel shifted attention away from its other problems. Mattel Electronics, once a star, turned into a dog. In 1982, there were over forty electronics products under development at Mattel. Only two came out on time. The management problems surfacing in this major unit didn't inspire confidence in Mattel's ability to handle a very diversified, unrelated set of businesses.

Even as well-managed a company as Sears takes its lumps occasionally. Sears World Trade was organized originally as a super-trading unit, capable of providing financial and consulting services to traders anywhere in the world. This ambitious scheme didn't fare too well. Now a new and less ambitious proposal to trim back to Sears's area of expertise is underway, using Sears's overseas offices and contacts to service Sears and other retailers.

Goethe said: "All intelligent thoughts have already been thought. What is necessary is only to try to think them again." The principle of distinctive competence has been around for some time. Like many ideas of strategy, it merely needs to be rediscovered. Completely new inventions are not nearly as important to strategy as understanding and implementing those that are already known.

KNOW YOUR *OWN* BUSINESS

The advantage in knowing how a business works is obvious if you are diversifying into it. Yet an equally compelling motive to become informed is if outsiders are diversifying into your business. Imagine, for example, the dilemma of established firms in the rapidly transforming business of financial services. Not only must they fend off new competitors, but they must also reevaluate their old strategies in light of changing circumstances. Where are the fights for advantage going to be won or lost? Assuming these leverage points are correctly perceived, what distinctive competence can each company bring to bear to exert maximum competitive pressure?

Speculating on the first point, distribution seems a logical major battleground for gaining competitive advantage. For mass marketers, anyway, reaching the customers comes first. In this struggle, large companies are coming at it from different directions and starting with different distinctive competences. The following table shows five of the "majors," each with a different core skill.

Sears and American Express have been the most ambitious diversifiers, while Equitable Life Assurance has just begun. The good news is that each acquisition enlarges the acquiror's share of the market. The bad news is that integrating unfamiliar and culturally different kinds of companies is troublesome. American Express and Sears already have encountered difficulties on this score. Merrill Lynch, on the other hand, is hamstrung by a brokerage system cemented in place. Its thousands of brokers are a great strength, but also a major deterrent to innovation. Discount brokers continue to take more and more share, and Merrill Lynch has been unable to move in a significant way from its traditional stance without alienating them. Not unlike the predicament faced by auto makers, losing the big car market (or big customers in Merrill Lynch's case) dissuades aggressive moves against competitors who come in at the bottom. And like the auto makers, the lost share to discount brokers has now grown to a point where action probably will be forced; an action that would have been more effective if Merrill Lynch had moved earlier.

All five companies in our table enjoy consumer trust, an immensely valuable commodity in selling financial services. One or the other company may have an edge in product or service specialization, but expertise marketed in volume is not that hard to acquire or imitate. The conclusion that distribution will make the difference seems hard to avoid. This may be what Walter Wriston, the former CEO of Citibank, perceived more than a decade ago when he predicted that his major competitor would not be another bank but Sears, Roebuck & Company.

Five Major Participants in a Burgeoning Financial Services Business

Company	Core Skill	Acquired Major Financial Services
American Express	Credit cards	Retail securities broker International banking firm
Citicorp	Commercial banking	None
Equitable	Life insurance	Institutional securities broker
Merrill Lynch	Securities broker	None
Sears	Retailing and insurance	Retail securities broker Real estate broker

Trying to peer into the future of financial services from a distance is an impossible task. Even from the inside, there are more questions than answers. But the decisions are unavoidable. The quality of moves made yesterday and in the near future will influence the final outcomes. Which companies prove to have the right stuff depends to a large extent on how well they have prepared. Who has done the best job of unravelling the keys to consumers' wants? On this score, a distant and analytical perspective with emphasis on the numbers alone will not be enough.

9 THE ROAD AHEAD

A S I AM WRITING this last chapter, it is early May 1985. By the time this book is published it will be 1986. In the interim, a lot may change. During the eighteen months or so this book took to research and write, a number of revisions were forced by events.

For example, Textron was my first choice to illustrate a transitional company that was focusing its efforts away from further diversification and toward management of its already far-flung enterprises. Then Textron acquired Avco and began another major round of restructuring.

The boards of National Intergroup and Bergen Brunswig both had approved the merger that would have taken National even further from its basic steel business, and would have provided me with a classic case of escape from a declining industry. But the deal fell through at the last minute. Even as I'm writing, General Electric is rumored to be a possible friendly buyer of CBS, if Ted Turner or other unwanted suitors appear successful in their takeover attempts. And Roger Smith, the chairman of General Motors, has hinted at a $1-billion surprise, possibly an unrelated acquisition, that may be in the car company's future. If one can't rely on the stability of GE and GM, is any prediction safe?

By the end, very little surprised me anymore. My own experiences reinforced the major lesson of this book: change is relentless. Yesterday's cases may not be there to illustrate tomorrow's story.

The basic motivations of management, however, tend to remain intact. Throughout the history of big business, managers have aimed for growth and control of markets. These pressures on management have been part of every major move forward, from small to large businesses, from large to related, and from related to unrelated.

Accepting these motivations as constant can enable us to see the legitimacy of the current strategy of unrelated diversification, and offer us new perspectives on the future of big business. The eight trends below, for instance, provide alternatives to the opinions of those who comment on business, rather than those who practice it. These trends rely on businesses' own past actions and motives as a means of anticipating what's coming next.

In large part, the trends below are an extension of the evidence of changes already noted in previous chapters. There are no major surprises or heroic forecasts. The major purpose is to stimulate further thought on unrelated diversification, instead of proving it good or bad.

Diversity Among U.S. Firms Will Continue Rising

The nation is in the midst of an industrial cycle. The trend that began after World War II is still in place because the motivations of change still exist. To reverse it would require shifts in managerial motives or strict government regulation of unrelated mergers. Neither seems likely at this time.

With the strategy of unrelated diversification now accepted by big businesses, companies still face a long period of refining its implementation and management. This suggests backing and filling as some firms divest themselves of unsuccessful past moves while others are just contemplating their first major unrelated acquisition. Individual cases of deconglomerating will thus be available, but the evidence in total indisputably supports the general move to more rather than less diversification.

Even holdouts like Polaroid and Eastman Kodak have discovered the risks of one-industry concentration and are moving to diversify away from total dependence on their core business. Once in motion, giant firms like these cannot achieve the optimum benefits of diversification with a single or even a few moves. The size of their initial base generally means several business groups are needed to create a balanced multi-business enterprise. Are Coke and Sears through with diversification? If they were, it would place them far short of competitive power in their new businesses.

It is the potential from the newly committed, partially committed, or as yet uncommitted diversifiers that will give the conglomerate movement its continued thrust. Only a minority of companies have taken a whole-hearted approach to unrelated diversification. This leaves a long path ahead for a great many companies before this unfamiliar strategy is assimilated and mastered by business as a whole.

Global Diversification Will Also Rise

Unrelated diversification is an economic rather than a national phenomenon. The same pressures that act on U.S. managers also influence managers of foreign companies. These forces can no more be restrained within a single country than expansion in the United States was able to be confined to particular industries.

The plain fact is that at some point growth in major markets becomes insufficient to accomodate giant companies that want to keep growing. To meet the demands for ever-rising revenues in saturated world markets, companies must either consolidate or grow outside of their core businesses. Both outcomes are likely to become more pronounced in the future, particularly among companies in mature industries.

In the domestic oil business, for example, what seemed to be insurmountable legal barriers to consolidations were quietly lowered as Texaco bought Getty, Mobil acquired Superior Oil, and Standard Oil of California purchased Gulf. But even this level of consolidation cannot satisfy growth pressures indefinitely. Combinations between foreign oil companies is a logical further step, paralleling the giant industry consolidations in the United States at the turn of the century.

Nestle's acquisition of the Carnation Company in 1984 is an example of this trend in the food business. Similar industry consolidations can be predicted in such major industries as automobiles, chemicals, and steel.

The formation of major global conglomerates can also be predicted, given the current trends in the U.S., and an assumption that the motives of managements will remain unchanged. Unrelated diversification becomes the best, and perhaps the only, alternative for companies in mature and labor-intensive industries in industrialized countries — with large cost disadvantages relative to companies in less developed countries — to assure their survival.

The history of modern business strategy up to now has been a case of the U.S. leading and the rest of the world following. This may change as the relative economic power and influence of the U.S. wanes. But the concept of unrelated diversification has already been demonstrated and its acceptance as a global strategy has been set in motion.

Reforms Will Be Forthcoming

Financial raiders like Pickens, Steinberg, Icahn, and Jacobs have given takeovers a tarnished image. No one could have imagined that companies like Disney, Texaco, and CBS would be fearful of individual investors buying them. But through a combination of gambler's nerves and eager lenders, it is no longer necessary to actually acquire a company in order to engage in takeover tactics. Financial entrepreneurs need only buy a stake in a company and then either extract "greenmail" as payment for going away, or make it a vulnerable target for other companies or raiders to buy.

In order to defend themselves, more and more companies are trying to make the cost of a takeover prohibitively expensive or difficult, or else grant top management "golden parachutes" so that a takeover, if it comes, will be immensely profitable for them. The eruption of such objectionable tactics like greenmail, poison pills, and golden parachutes has gotten to the point where public reaction is inevitable. Congress and the Securities and Exchange Commission are both engaged in hearings on reforms. Even persons in the merger business appear to favor restraint of the more abusive takeover maneuvers.

Curbing the excesses of financial takeover artists does not mean that mergers will stop, although the pace may slow for a while. In the merger wave of the 1960s, reforms of accounting rules eliminated a patent abuse but proved healthy for mergers in the long run. Similarly, the point has probably been reached where the entire merger movement will benefit if the feverish pitch of speculation is cooled down.

Sensible reforms are not contradictory to a basically free market for acquisitions. Acquiring underutilized assests, and even liquidating obsolete assets is part of the reindustrialization of America. But any new opportunity for huge profits has always stimulated regulation that defined the rules for fair play. In this case, the feeling has been growing that the capital markets are being manipulated for the benefit of a few. In the process, companies are dismembered or their balance sheets encumbered with debt, without concern for any basic improvements in the company itself.

When the economy is expanding, the growth covers up such excesses until they become catastrophic. Acting now can help to avoid the worst of the hangover that will follow an unchecked build-up of speculation. The delicate part of reforms will be to cut out the undesirable practices without stopping the merger movement altogether.

Operating Synergies Will Determine Long-Term Winners

Over the long haul, the most successful bidders will be those firms that successfully integrate their acquisitions. This applies to all acquisitions, including unrelated ones. It is a trend that was observable in prior evolutionary stages in the history of big business. It is still applicable to today's conglomerates.

Companies that have tried to operate their acquisitions as a portfolio of investments have been those most exposed to asset-stripping. Financial raiders like those mentioned above have honed in on firms whose pieces are likely to be worth more to someone who can actively and more profitably operate them than when they are held as arm's-length businesses. By borrowing the money to buy such companies and then selling off the parts, a raider can in effect bootstrap the purchase with the company's own assets.

Realizing the dangers of sitting on nonperforming investments, more companies have begun to reevaluate their strategy. If the raiders can move profits for themselves, why not capture the benefits for the company and its shareholders directly?

Oil companies like ARCO and Mobil have been two major examples of this approach. Neither has been particularly successful in its nonoil acquisitions. Exxon is also looking to get out of the office equipment field, while Texaco has shed a number of unrelated acquisitions. This is a case in which an entire industry went on a merger binge without a clear idea for post-acquisition management. It has taken considerable time, and declining fortunes in the oil business, before the realization sank in that these assets are worth more to others than to themselves.

On the other hand, oil companies have not repudiated mergers. On the contrary, they have introduced a new era of megamergers in the oil business. At this point in their evolution, oil companies seem destined to consolidate rather than diversify. This process accomplishes the primary goals of growth and market control while avoiding the handicap of getting into businesses oil companies are not prepared to run.

Disappointing results by companies that have tried to operate unrelated acquisitions from a distance confirms the notion of establishing a distinctive competence as the basis for a successful diversification policy. The more operational connections that can be built between two companies — even though they operate in different businesses — the more potential there is for long-term synergy. By not knowing the retail business, or failing to know it intimately later, Mobil found that its purchase of Montgomery Ward never justified the investment poured into it. Montgomery Ward eventually became an anchor on earnings that Mobil could not justify.

Only by imparting value to an acquisition can its full potential be realized. In the absence of such synergy, companies must rely on receiving the same financial returns that the acquired company could have generated had it been left independent. As has been demonstrated, there is justification for such acquisitions under the right circumstances, but they generally offer the fewest benefits.

In the industrial restructuring now taking place, the switching of assets is in part a recognition of the misalignments that have accumulated over the past. New acquirors are also learning from past mistakes and taking a more reasoned approach to unrelated diversification. This Darwinian process of natural selection and divestitures should accrue to the benefit of the nation as a whole as operational excellence improves overall.

Unrelated Diversification Will be Forced, As Well as Planned

Dr. Henry Singleton of Teledyne commented that the principal reason companies diversify is "the natural desire of companies to survive." And for some, diversification is an alternative forced by circumstances. They find themselves in terminally ill situations, as did basic steel, and diversification is the most feasible path to follow. U.S. Steel, for example, now receives more than half of its revenues from oil and gas.

In other cases, companies that pursue a single-purpose strategy beyond the point of diminishing returns must either diversify or stagnate. Polaroid, for instance, is still identified with amateur instant photography. Possessed with a desire for innovation, Polaroid had committed itself deeper and deeper into this one business. Concurrently, its paternalistic guarantee of lifetime employment bloated its workforce. Ultimately, the combination of a narrow specialization, increasing competition, and an unproductive workforce humbled this once-proud company. In an effort to dig its way out of this hole, it has ventured into nonconsumer photographic applications, and is dabbling in less related areas like computer products, video equipment, and electronic imaging.

Polaroid's is not a classic way to diversify. It delayed acting until it was forced to react. The choice of diversification, in this case, was made for the wrong reason.

But the choice of strategy is seldom as carefully planned as in the textbooks on strategy. A common image of decision-making depicts it as a very rational process of anticipation and proaction. In fact, examination has shown that managers rely heavily on intuition, experience, and the guidance of their chief executive. The end result can be fortuitous, even if not planned.

Take Xerox, for example. In 1969, it acquired Scientific Data Systems (SDS), a computer company. Soon after its purchase, it was seen as a disaster. Xerox had overpaid and the company never came up to expectations. However, SDS provided Xerox with the technology for its eventual thrust into computer-assisted office equipment. It took Xerox over a decade to reap the benefits from its earlier diversification decision. In retrospect, this decision probably helped Xerox to avoid the situation in which Polaroid now finds itself.

Other companies will follow the diversification paths of either a U.S. Steel, Polaroid, or Xerox. Pressured by industry circumstances, past strategic errors, or prior experience, more companies will see diversification as the least risky of their options. In effect, the emphasis on survival — and profits — will ensure not only that diversification continues but that more companies will go farther, if not divorce themselves altogether, from the markets in which they first began to do business.

The People Side of Management Will Get More Attention

Are there better ways to communicate in organizations that employ thousands of workers? A number of companies for the first time are trying innovative techniques. One General Motors executive, for example, employs a "diagonal slice," whereby he meets with a randomly chosen group of employees, including middle managers and assembly-line workers.

The chairman of General Motors, Roger Smith, has worked hard to push decision-making power lower and loosen the chain of command. In a two-year exhaustive study commissioned by General Motors, McKinsey & Co. found that the company had become risk-averse. Managers were afraid to take chances. Routine had become habit. Moreover, as in other multi-layered firms, the decision-making process had become time-consuming and cumbersome. In essence, General Motors' management had come to resemble a vast white-collar assembly line; even minor questions had to travel from one end to the other before a decision could be reached. As part of the solution, a participative style of management was installed. Bosses became more accessible to subordinates and workers contributed more to decision-making. And if General Motors can change, any organization can change.

The traditional philosophy that has kept management and workers in opposite camps, with emphasis on impersonal financial management rather than personal contacts, is showing signs of erosion. Prodded by the success of the Japanese, American manufacturers have adopted their own versions of "quality circles," where employees work in tandem and for common goals. They hope not only to improve employee relations, but to raise productivity — and profits — as well.

These moves could be just another fad, of course, characterized by many books on the subject and a few corporate experiments. With the economy bouncing back, the pressure for innovative solutions could diminish. Companies would then feel free to return to business as usual.

This time, however, two counterforces are at work to keep the emphasis on participatory management. The first is the continued pressure of the Japanese. They are not only exporting their goods, they also are exporting their management practices. Along with building more plants in the United States, they are running them with their particular brand of people management. The advantages of this management style can provide a competitive edge as long as it remains a monopoly of the Japanese.

On a broader scale, the push for bettter communications with employees should come unilaterally from U.S. managements seeking to instill more entrepreneurial spirit in their businesses. In too many instances, acquired business groups have been given autonomy, but decision-making within each group remains highly formalized.

The objective of better people management, under the guise of participatory management or quality circles or whatever, should be to achieve *true* decentralization. Each business unit should be able to react flexibly and quickly to its competition. This requires building communication networks within each distinct business. If companies can recapture the esprit and risk-taking attitudes that small size affords, they can retain the benefits of consolidating many such businesses under one structure. And although this is a paramount challenge for conglomerates, it is a problem that affects any large company. It is, in fact, the very pervasiveness of the problem, and the reported instances of progress in solving it, that ensure the momentum for fundamental changes will build.

"Maximization of Shareholders' Interests" Needs to be Rethought

Acting to maximize benefits to shareowners has become a conditioned response to the question of where management's responsibilities lie. But which shareowner groups' interests are to be maximized, and what are their legitimate claims on the company?

The concept of "shareowners' interests" has become fuzzier as ownership has increasingly shifted to institutional investors. "The problem is deciding who the hell the corporation is responsible to," says the CEO of Champion International. "I can't ask my shareholders what .they want. Champion is 75 percent owned by institutions, and many shareholders change so damn fast I don't even know who they are." Besides, he adds, "We're owned by a bunch of index funds [a mechanical approach to selecting stocks]. Who votes for an index fund? Some mathematical formula votes your stock."

Although the ownership of public companies has moved from owner-entrepreneurs to individual investors and increasingly towards institutional investors, the validity of maximizing shareowners' interests has never undergone serious scrutiny. Professional managers have been put in a position of trying to satisfy a shifting constituency. Whatever they do, they can be subject to the claim that they are not acting in a specific shareowner group's best interests. As discussed in Chapter 2, critics of unrelated acquisitions have argued that companies should leave diversification to their shareholders and stick to the business they know. It has made little impression on them that this amounts to a prescription for disaster if applied rigidly in every situation.

Once the separation between ownership and management became the rule for public companies, the identification of shareholders' interests with managerial actions could no longer be assumed. It still applies some of the time. It may even pertain as a broad general statement. But the time is past when one can naively assume that interests of specific shareholder groups necessarily coincide with objective economic criteria for consumer welfare in general.

Are corporate raiders like T. Boone Pickens, a self-proclaimed protector of shareholder interests, really acting for the greater good? When such raiders are paid greenmail, doesn't that money come from the pockets of the shareholders in order to enrich the raider? Are arbitrageurs, who come in just after takeover rumors begin and depart right after a merger, the type of shareholders who deserve protection?

These are not easy questions to answer. Managers and shareowners obviously share some common goals but are just as clearly motivated by differing self-interests. The only certainty is that a proper resolution between these two main parties is not as simplistic as the slogan "let the interests of the shareowners decide."

Conglomerates Will Continue to Get a Cool Reception from Educators

The safest assumption about the future is that resistance to unrelated diversification will persist. Although the notion of change is an absorbing subject for intellectual debate, the inertia working for retention of conventional ideas is very strong. Intellectual commitments have been made. Models of how things should work have been carefully defined. Minor exceptions can be taken as progress, but dramatic departures are looked on as heresy.

Where conglomerates are concerned, the idea that unrelated diversification makes economic sense flies in the face of economic principles that say otherwise. Economists have a very specific explanation of mergers: they should raise efficiency by lowering costs. When one company buys another, economic benefits arise only if the two companies have joint costs that can be lowered by merging. Since in a conglomerate acquisition there are no cost overlaps to eliminate, there are theoretically no economic benefits to reap.

Experience, however, has proven to be the mother of invention in the case of conglomerates. Driven by practical needs, managers have not found diversification into unrelated businesses to be as unrewarding, or as catastrophic, as predicted. With continued experimentation and persistence, the logic of diversifying into new businesses has become more compelling for an ever increasing number of companies.

Meanwhile, the rewards of "shared costs" have proved elusive. Managers have found the concept difficult to implement, even though it continues to be marketed as good theory. Walter Kiechel III, an editor of *Fortune*, provides an anecdotal insight into the rift between scientific prescriptions and pragmatic needs:

In 1979 I asked several consulting firms what were the new, key concepts of strategy? The only new one they had to offer was the idea of shared costs. This is the notion that if you analyzed the components of your products you might realize there was one component you were putting into all of them, and that you were getting good experience-curve cost reduction in the manufacture of that component so you better be careful about getting rid of any of the products.

Actually, this concept had initially been thought up by George Bennett and others when they were at BCG working on a case at Texas Instruments. So I went back to Texas Instruments, where the idea originated, to ask, "How do you use the share cost idea?" They said, "It was a little too complicated for our line managers. We didn't use it."[1]

Igor Ansoff, one of the early writers on business strategy, once commented on the probability that "the historical lag of education behind practice will persist." At an earlier time, I believed that assessment was unduly pessimistic. I am no longer sure. There are natural advantages for educators in a precisely calculatable model of how companies *should* behave. Based on the conglomerate record, if educators are given the choice between revising theory and proving that no revision is necessary, a majority will get busy on the proof.

Notes

1. Walter Kiechel III, "Sniping At Strategic Planning," *Planning Review*, May 1984, p. 9.

INDEX